TOWARDS
A
READING-WRITING
CLASSROOM

TOWARDS
A
READING-WRITING
CLASSROOM

Andrea Butler
Jan Turbill

Primary English Teaching Association
NSW, Australia

Heinemann
Portsmouth, New Hampshire

HEINEMANN EDUCATIONAL BOOKS, INC.
361 Hanover Street
Portsmouth, NH 03801
Offices and agents throughout the world

First U.S. printing 1987

Library of Congress Cataloging-in-Publication Data

Butler, Andrea.
    Towards a reading-writing classroom.

Reprint. Originally published: Rozelle, NSW: Primary English Teaching Association, 1984.
    Bibliography: p.
    Includes index.
    1. English language—Composition and Exercises—Study and teaching. 2. Reading (Elementary)—Language experience approach.
I. Turbill, Jan. II. Title.
LB1576.B96 1988   372.6   87-29663
ISBN 0-435-08461-5

Acknowledgements

The authors and publisher are grateful to the following for permission to reproduce copyright material: Ashton Scholastic (*I Think I'm in Trouble*); Martin Bailey (*The Big Toe*); Joy Cowley and June Melser (*Smarty Pants* and *The Big Toe*); Ted Greenwood (*Everlasting Circle*); Murray Grimsdale (*Smarty Pants*); Roger Haldane and Colin Thiele (*Magpie Island*); Lorraine Wilson and Thomas Nelson Australia (*And the Teacher Got Mad*).

Advisory Panel

Dr Elaine Furniss
St George Institute,
Sydney College of Advanced Education

Viv Nicoll
Macarthur Institute of Higher Education (NSW)

Robyn Platt
Grays Point Public School (NSW)

Keith Pigdon
Melbourne College of Advanced Education

Di Snowball
Phillip Institute of Technology (Vic.)

Lorraine Wilson
Author and Language Consultant (Vic.)

Marilyn Woolley
Melbourne College of Advanced Education

Printed in the United States of America
10 9 8 7 6 5 4

Contents

Preface

In a little village on the North Coast of NSW two PETA books have already been written. It was in the same setting during the 1983-84 Christmas vacation that we began this book. We foolishly thought it would be finished within two weeks. Many Saturdays and one long Easter vacation finally saw the last words written. But none of it would have been possible without the generous assistance, enthusiasm and ideas of many people.

We wish to thank the members of the advisory panel who helped us form the outline of the book, conferred with us, and read our final draft. We are very grateful for their comments. We particularly want to thank our Melbourne friends who took us to many schools, and gave us many ideas. Thanks, too, to Dr Brian Cambourne (University of Wollongong) who provided us with inspiration and a theoretical framework. We would also like to thank Marilyn Woolley and Keith Pigdon (Melbourne College of Advanced Education) for their contribution both in writing and in assistance with the photography. Two Victorian primary schools which provided us with a great deal of inspiration were Moonee Ponds West and Deer Park North. We are grateful to both staff and children. Lastly, we would like to thank all those teachers who often unknowingly have shared their experiences with us. We are both in the fortunate position of having met and observed many teachers and children in many schools throughout Australia and New Zealand. They have taught us much about the teaching of reading and writing. We have written this book in the hope that it will inspire more teachers to move towards a reading-writing classroom.

Jan Turbill and Andrea Butler.

Dedicated to Andy and Miffy.

PART 1
THEORETICAL BACKGROUND

Chapter 1
Introduction

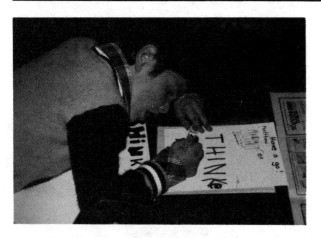

"Good, isn't it?" said Matthew, pleased with the piece of writing he had just completed.

Matthew is only six but already he believes he is a successful reader and writer. Similar confidence is displayed by his 28 fellow students, who are all members of a stimulating **reading-writing** classroom.

The teaching of writing in Australian and New Zealand schools has undergone exciting changes as more and more teachers have become aware of the great benefits of adopting a "process-conference" approach. They have realised that once the act of writing is seen as a process (rather than a product)

then it makes sense to allow children to write creatively as professional authors do, through a process which includes drafting, revising, editing and polishing, with possible publication (and therefore an audience) in view.

The children in Matthew's class have confidence in themselves because this is the approach used by their teacher. However, this teacher does not see writing as a discrete "subject" but wisely links it to reading—which is also seen as a process—integrating both parts within the total language program, and the curriculum generally.

As a natural consequence of the growth of the "process-conference" approach to writing, the authors of this book have sought out a number of teachers, throughout Australia and New Zealand, who are developing truly integrated reading-writing classrooms. We have visited their schools to observe them in action and have been drawn into participating in reading-writing activities within them. That is how we happened to meet six-year-old Matthew.

On the day we visited Matthew's classroom to take photographs for this book, he was sitting at a table designing the cover for the book he was about to write. We sat down beside him to photograph some children at work on the other side of the room. Matthew took very little notice of us at first. He finished the design and began to write, saying each word slowly as he wrote it: "I . . . think . . . I'm . . . in . . .". He stopped writing and reached for a piece of cardboard labelled "Have a Go". On this card he tried writing *trouble*. He wrote *trubl*; then, turning to us, he stated: "That's not right, is it?"

"No," we agreed. "Try writing it again on your card."

This time he added an *e* to the end and then carefully sounded the word again. "T-a-r-uble", he said slowly, writing an *a* in between the *t* and the *r*. "Is that right now?" he asked, and added quickly: "It doesn't look right."

"What part doesn't look right?"

He pointed to the *a* in *taruble* and said: "That's not right," and then, pointing to *truble*, said, "Oh, I remember now."

Before we could say any more he crossed out the *a* and inserted the *o* in the correct position. He had tried the word three times before being finally happy with it. Without further conversation he copied *trouble* onto his cover. Holding it up in front of himself he said to nobody in particular: "Good, isn't it?"

We asked him where he got the idea for the book.

"Our teacher read that book (pointing to a small book *I Think I'm in Trouble* resting on the chalkboard ledge) to my group yesterday and then we read it too. It's about these kids who do all these things but they know they'll get in trouble so they say: 'How was I supposed to know?' Our teacher and us wrote our own book like it. See, it's over there on the wall."

We looked over to where he was pointing and could see cardboard sheets containing what appeared to be a draft story.

"Those kids there (pointing to a group we'd been photographing) are drawing the pictures to go with the stories we did, and then my teacher will make it into a 'big book'. But I'm going to do my own book all by myself."

With that, Matthew took a fresh sheet of paper and began to write, saying each word carefully: "I left the lite on and all the elertriserty ran aot". He drew a bubble around *aot*. When we asked why he did this, he said that he was not sure if that word was right or not, so the bubble will let his teacher know that he wants to know about that word.

"What about *electricity*?" we asked.

"Oh, I know that's wrong, but that doesn't matter, you know."

Taking another sheet of paper, he asked if we could help him. "This is going to be a long story, so you can write some. You can write: 'I left the tap on and all the water ran out', and I'll write: 'How was I supposed to know?' on this other one. O.K.?"

Quite bemused, we did as told. When we had finished, Matthew took the sheet and read it through. "You left something out," he said. We had done as instructed but he expected us to realise that he wanted more, so, taking the coloured pencil from my hand, he wrote *in the barth room*, above the word *on*. "I'll write the rest," he said, and proceeded to write: "How was I suposed (supposed) to noe (know)?" Obviously he didn't trust us to write more!

Matthew went on to write two more pages for his book. Some words he tried out on his "Have a Go" card until they were correct; others he drew bubbles around and others he left. All the words he placed bubbles around had close to conventional spelling. He continually read and re-read his work to himself and his friends at the same table. At a later stage he would work through the piece with his teacher, checking on meaning and eventually on the words with the bubbles. These words would then be copied into a personal dictionary for later reference. His story would be copied out by his teacher onto sheets of coloured paper which Matthew would choose. His own book would sit alongside the commercially-produced book which had been his model.

Six-year-old Matthew is already a confident writer.

Cover and sample page from the Ashton Scholastic book used as Matthew's model.

For Matthew, reading, writing and spelling are being learnt in an integrated and meaningful context as naturally as the one in which he acquired the ability to talk. What is happening in this classroom—and many others—we have found so exciting, rewarding and meaningful for both children and teachers that we have compiled this book, incorporating into it statements from the teachers themselves, in order to spread the word about reading-writing classrooms with teachers everywhere.

Starting from Dr Brian Cambourne's theory about favourable conditions under which children learn to speak, we go on to outline a theoretical framework before describing the practical ways in which teachers are encouraging children like Matthew to read and write in similarly favourable conditions and in a truly integrated way. It is our hope that this book will lead more teachers to move towards establishing similarly productive, happy and stimulating reading-writing classrooms in their own schools.

Chapter 2
Language, learning and literacy

Another way of looking at language learning

Brian Cambourne
Centre for Studies in Literacy
University of Wollongong

What comes to mind when you hear or read the phrase "language learning"? If you are like the typical teacher or student to whom I put this question, the picture you get in your mind is one of a young child learning how to use the oral mode of the language of his/her culture, i.e. learning how to talk. Very rarely when I ask this question (and I ask it of as many teachers as I possibly can) do I get a response which suggests that "language learning" also includes learning how to use the written form of language, i.e. learning how to read and write.

Why? I have discussed this issue with so many teachers that for me the reason is obvious: the majority of teachers and students to whom I have put the question make the assumption that the written form of language is significantly different from the oral form. Not only do they believe it to be a secondary, more abstract, form of language, but they believe that the brain processes it differently and that it is learned quite differently.

Although there are many consequences of thinking about oral and written language in this way which spill over into classroom teaching practices, one in particular stands out: teachers who hold these beliefs are subtly diverted from considering how the principles which underpin one very successful example of language learning (i.e. learning how to mean in the oral mode) might also apply to another example of language learning (i.e. learning how to mean in the written mode).

Let us consider the phenomenon of learning to talk. It is not difficult to argue that it is a very impressive learning feat. In fact, learning to speak the language of the culture into which one is born is without doubt the most spectacular single learning enterprise that anyone ever sets out to undertake. How would you, an adult in control of one language at least, like to start learning a language like Japanese, Swahili, Hebrew, Urdu, Kakikiutl, or any of the three to four thousand living languages spoken on earth today? You would find it to be an immensely difficult and complex task. Every language consists of a unique set of thousands of "conventions" organised in extremely complex but arbitrary ways, with idiosyncratic grammars, phonemic and morphemic structures, pragmatic dimensions, etc. Yet there are millions of toddlers, with very "immature" brains, successfully learning these complex languages at this very minute, with remarkable ease. What is more, they will have most of the really complex bits learned by the time they are 5½ or 6½. If they are "normal" children, they'll have "mental ages" which are roughly equivalent to their chronological ages, i.e. 5½-6½. Where would you be if you had a mental age of 5½-6½? You certainly would not be reading this book. (In fact, as an adult, you would probably be under custody.) Yet all over the world little children are learning something as complex as the language of their culture—and have been doing so for countless thousands of years.

How do they do it?

I believe that the conditions which operate when this learning takes place have something to do with it. I realise that linguistic researchers have shown that humans have been specially programmed ("wired") by the Director of the Universe (whoever *She* is) to learn language. This is true, yet certain human beings who, for some reason or other, are denied the conditions that operate when normal children learn to talk (e.g. "feral" children like the Wild Boy of Averyon, or more recently the case of "Genie" in the USA), fail to learn any language at all. This strongly suggests that there is more to learning to talk than merely having been "wired" neurologically in a certain way.

The evidence is, I believe, conclusive: in order to learn to talk one must not only be human, but certain conditions must operate to permit that learn-ing to occur. These conditions are many and complex but, I believe, there are seven that stand out. I also believe that these seven conditions are relevant to all kinds of language learning, e.g. learning to read, write, spell; learning a second language. Furthermore, I believe that these conditions are transferable to classroom practice.

Conditions under which children learn to talk

In what follows, I'm going to discuss each one of the seven conditions which I believe help learning "how to mean in the oral mode of language" (i.e. talking) so universally successful. After each section you should ask yourself the question which follows, and consider your own answers in the light of what I have written.

Condition 1: Immersion

From the moment they are born, meaningful spoken language washes over and surrounds children. They are *immersed* in a "language flood" and, for most of their waking time, proficient users of the language-culture that they happen to have been born into literally bathe them in the sounds, meanings, cadences and rhythms of the language that they have to learn. It is important to realise that this language which continually flows around them is always meaningful, usually purposeful and, more importantly, *whole*. (In the real world, people don't usually talk nonsense; nor do they talk using fragments of the language.)

Question: *What does this mean for learning to use the* **print** *medium? For learning to read, write, spell?*

Condition 2: Demonstration

Demonstration is a term I have borrowed from Frank Smith. A close synonym is the term "model". By it I mean that children, in the process of learning to talk, receive thousands and thousands of demonstrations (models or examples) of the spoken form of the language being used in functional and meaningful ways. The child sitting in the high chair at breakfast hears a stream of sounds emitted from his father's mouth—and the sugar bowl is passed across. This kind of "demonstration" of the conventions which are used to express meanings is repeated over and over again, and through them the learner is given the data which enables him to adopt the conventions that he needs to use in order to be a speaker/comprehender of the language culture into which he has been born.

Question: *What kinds of "demonstrations" are typically provided for young learners wanting to grasp the conventions that make the* **written** *medium "comprehensible"? Are they of this kind?*

Condition 3: Expectation

Lately, I have been asking parents of new-born babies a question which always brings a puzzled response. (They think I'm some kind of nut.) After congratulating them on producing such a marvellous example of humanity, I slip in this question:

"Do you expect him/her to learn to talk?"
Try it sometime. Unless the infant is really severely damaged, you will find that all parents *expect* their children to learn to talk. Expectations, I believe, are very subtle forms of communication, to which learners respond. We "give off" expectations that our children will learn to walk and talk, and they do, even though it's quite often painful (walking) and very complicated (talking).

Next time there's a vacation swimming school on near your home, spend some time observing the kinds of expectations about swimming that the parents give off. "It's hard", "It's dangerous", "You'll never do it", are the messages that the body language, the gestures, and the things actually said, communicate to many of these children. And how do they respond? How many of us actually expect our teenage children not to learn to drive? How many of them fail to do it? If we give off the expectation that learning to read, write, spell, talk another language is difficult, complex, beyond children, then many of them will respond accordingly. The kids in the "Wombat" group will read, spell, write and talk like wombats if we expect them to.

Question: *How many ways can we give children the expectation that learning language-based skills is "difficult", "complex", "beyond children"?*

Condition 4: Responsibility

When learning to talk, children are left to take *responsibility* for what they learn about their language. No parents ever say: "Our pride and joy has not learned the passive/negative transformation yet. So for the next five weeks we'll teach him that. Then we'd better get onto the embeddings involving relativisation and adverbial conjoiners." They let the *child* decide which set of conventions to master.

Until my wife stopped me using them as guinea pigs, I monitored my children's language development carefully, especially during the toddler stage. (My wife is eminently sensible when it comes to child raising. She had to teach me to differentiate between the roles of father and researcher.) They mastered different grammatical structures at different ages. What is important is that they arrived at the same state of language "know-how" at about

5½-6½. Like children everywhere, they arrived at the same destination by different routes. This is natural learning. If we tried to take that responsibility away, our children would not learn to talk.

Question: *Do we typically extend the same privilege to learning how to comprehend/mean with the* **written** *medium?*

The pre-school child is constantly engaged in language learning in an encouraging environment.

Condition 5: Approximation

Young learners of the oral mode of a language (i.e. talking) are not expected to display full-blown adult competence from the beginning. Parents actually reward children not just for being *right*, but also for being *close*. *Example:* A toddler points to a cup on the table and says: "Dat Daddy cup." No parent ever responds by saying: "You stupid child. You left out the auxiliary (indicative mood) *is*

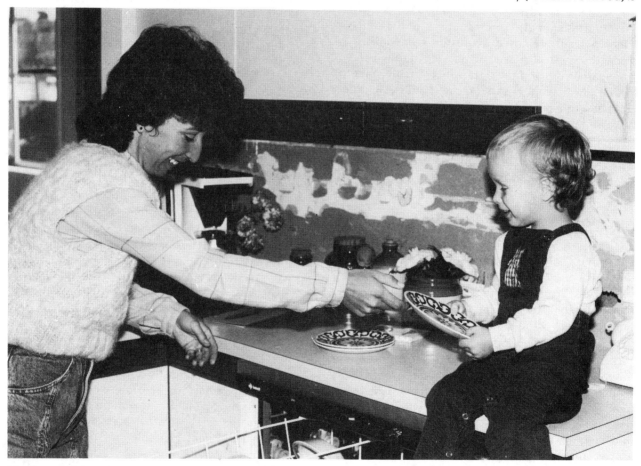

and the possessive 's and you mispronounced *that*. Now say after me: *'That is Daddy's cup'*."

How many children would want to go on with the task of learning to talk if this is how we treated them? Yet a common experience I have, as I talk with teachers and observe classroom activities, is that, with regard to the *written* mode of language, children are expected to display adult competence from the beginning. Countless times I have heard children corrected for reading *Daddy* when the text word was *Father*. There are not many schools where a young child's attempt to write "Once upon a time" as "WSAPNATM" would be tolerated. When I talk to parents or teachers about approximations, and ask them why they don't chastise a toddler for saying "Dat cup" instead of "That's a cup", they usually laugh. Yet they feel uncomfortable about children being given the same privileges with respect to the *written* language.

Question: *What theory of learning to read and spell do most teachers and parents have?*

Condition 6: Employment

Plenty of opportunity to *use* the medium is provided when learning to talk. We don't restrict our children to two twenty-minute periods per week to employ the conventions of spoken language, and prevent them from practising them at other times. We don't force them to wait until "talking-time" comes around each week.

Question: *What do we do when teaching children to read, write, spell?*

Condition 7: Feedback

How do our immature learners get from "Dat cup" to "That's a cup", from "Mummy sock?" to "Is that Mummy's sock?" I spent three years of my life "bugging" young children with a radio microphone in order to find answers to this and other questions. I sat half a mile up the road and picked up what they said, and what was said to them, from the time they woke up until the time they went to bed. I had field binoculars so that I could also observe and note the context in which language was used whenever they were outside. The evidence I have is quite conclusive, and is supported by other studies from other countries: the adults (and older siblings too) who teach young children give them feedback of a very special kind, e.g.

Toddler: *Dat cup.*
Adult: *Yes, that's a cup.*

The message is received ("Yes") and the conventional adult, expanded form is given back in a non-threatening, mean-centred way, e.g.

Toddler: *Yesterday, I GOED down town.*
Adult: *Yesterday, you WENT down town did you?*

Furthermore, no parents in my data (or anyone else's data) expected the child to produce the conventional adult form the very next time the child used it. They knew that the "baby" talk may persist for weeks, the *goed* and *fighted* and *comed* and other immature attempts at communication would continue until the **child** decided to change. No exasperated pressure of the kind: "Look, I've modelled the auxiliary a dozen times now—when will you get it right?" was ever given. I want to suggest that, unfortunately, the feedback we give children in school, with respect to the *written* form of the language, is not quite the same.

Question: *Why not? What must teachers believe about learning?*

Chapter 3
The reading-writing processes

How do proficient readers and writers go about the task of reading and writing? What are the similarities between the two processes and how do these processes integrate within the total language context? What does a reader learn about writing from reading? What does a writer learn about reading from writing? We shall address these questions in this chapter.

Reading and writing are both acts of composing. Readers, using their background of knowledge and experience, compose meaning from the text; writers, using their background of knowledge and experience, compose meaning into text. For both processes it is helpful to look at what readers and writers *do* in each of three different phases, i.e. *before* the act of reading and writing, *during* the act and *after* the act.

What Readers Do BEFORE Reading	What Writers Do BEFORE Writing
The proficient reader brings and uses knowledge: • about the topic (semantic knowledge) • about the language used (syntactic knowledge) • about the sound-symbol system (graphophonic knowledge)	The proficient writer brings and uses knowledge: • about the topic (semantic knowledge) • about the language to be used (syntactic knowledge) • about the sound-symbol system (graphophonic knowledge)
The proficient reader brings certain expectations to the reading cued by: • previous reading experiences • presentation of the text • the purpose for the reading • the audience for the reading	The proficient writer brings certain expectations based on: • previous writing experiences • previous reading experiences • the purpose of the writing • the audience for the writing

The expectations and prior knowledge the proficient readers and writers have will determine the manner in which they approach their tasks. The reader has expectations, and therefore makes predictions about the text, based on the presentation and visual cues. The purpose for reading becomes clarified and the desire to read increases or decreases.

The reader expects a newspaper to contain certain types of information arranged and presented in a certain way. These expectations are based on the type of newspapers the reader has read previously. Newspapers are organised differently according to their scope and subject areas, purpose and audience. A financial paper will differ from a sports paper; a sports magazine will be different again. Proficient readers make reasonable guesses about the expected content, style, etc. of these materials and choose accordingly. For example, the technical nature of the text in (b) may be of interest to the reader who has a background and interest in the area. To others, a quick glance might give enough information for them to be able to predict or conclude that the text is technical and of no interest.

Text (c) is obviously a story. The title and the amount of conversation (indicated by the punctuation) help readers to assume that it is a story or novel of some sort. The title gives the reader further information to predict what the piece might be about and whether it would be of interest or not.

Such expectations will have been formed by readers over time as they experience a wide range of text read for a variety of purposes. The *writer* will likewise have expectations as to how the text might develop and therefore will begin to consider questions such as:

- Why am I writing this?
- Who will be the reader (s)?
- Should the type of language used (register) be narrative, factual, humorous, or in the form of a report; should I develop an argument or use particular stylistic devices such as rhyme, dialect, rhythm?
- Do I know enough about the topic?
- Should I talk with someone about it?

---

a

Workers accept cut, save accord

By PAUL ROBINSON

Twenty-six furniture workers have agreed to take an $11.90 pay cut and about 220 ironworkers will get a total of $10,000 compensation in a deal which removes a big threat to the prices and incomes accord.

Union sources said yesterday that the Federal Government had threatened the Furnishing Trades Society with some form of deregistration unless 26 of their members abandoned a pay rise they won recently after a three-week strike at an aluminium window-making plant.

The threat to the accord came when the Federated Ironworkers' Association started a campaign for a flow-on. If this had been successful, the claim would have spread to thousands of metal-workers throughout Australia.

Under the deal reached this week, the 220 ironworkers will get

accord, the influence of the ACTU, and the determination of the Federal Government to bring into line unions that seek pay rises outside the national wage-fixing principles. The Government recognised that the claim was a threat to its national economic policy.

The deal also seems likely to see the Furnishing Trades Society being reimbursed, in full or in part, for money lost by its members in their strike to win the allowance at Dowell Australia Ltd.

The $48 payment to each of the ironworkers represents $6 a week for the past eight weeks. In that time, the 26 members of the Furnishing Trades Society received a $6 allowance payment.

The $6 was the first stage of the $11.90 agreement between the union and the company. That agreement has now lapsed.

The second stage $5.90, was due to be introduced from September

---

b

Brazing setup		Upper electrode	Lower electrode	Mol
			Electrode detail	

Conditions for Resistance Brazing

Machine ....Press-type, air-operated 75-kva resistance welding machine
Electrodes ....RWMA class 14 (molybdenum), water-cooled
Electrode force ....500 lb
Current ....55 amp
Voltage ....1.5 v

Filler metal ......BCuP-5 preform, ¼ by ⅛ in., by 0.005 in. thick(a)
Squeeze time ....70 cycles
Heating time ....114 cycles(b)
Hold time ....18 cycles
Off time, minimum ....120 cycles
Brazing time, per joint ....8 seconds

(a) Flux not used. (b) Six pulses, each of 11 cycles heating time plus 8 cycles cooling time.

Fig. 24. Assembly of armature leads to commutator bars, and setup for resistance brazing, which replaced staking and torch soldering, giving faster production and eliminating contamination and excessive annealing (Example 656)

satisfactory mechanical staking and torch soldering procedure that also produced unwanted heating effects.

Example 656. Resistance Brazing Instead of Torch Soldering for Lap-Joint Attachment of Armature Leads to Commutator Bars (Fig. 24)

The original method of making the commutator shown in Fig. 24 was to insert the alloy 110 armature leads into holes in the alloy 114 commutator bars, mechanically

and initial cost of equipment were major factors in the selection of resistance brazing for attaching dual armature leads to commutator bars.

Example 657. Resistance Brazing Instead of Carbon-Arc Brazing for Joining Armature Leads to Commutators (Fig. 25)

When carbon-arc brazing was used for joining alloy 102 armature leads to alloy 110 commutator bars (see Fig. 25), the joints

---

c

PRUDENT HANS

NE day, Hans's mother said,
" Where are you going, Hans ? "
Hans answered,
" To Grethel's, mother."
" Manage well, Hans."
" All right !   Good-bye, mother."
" Good-bye, Hans."
Then Hans came to Grethel's.
" Good morning, Grethel."

" Good morning, Hans.   What have you brought me day ? "

" I have brought nothing, but I want something."

So Grethel gave Hans a needle ; and then he said,

" Good-bye, Grethel," and she said, " Good-bye, Hans.

Hans carried the needle away with him, and stuck it i hay-cart that was going along, and he followed it home.

" Good evening, mother."

" Good evening, Hans.   Where have you been ? "

- How will I set it out? What is the best way to say it?
- Shall I use pictures, words, or both?

Decisions will be made by the writer, based on past experiences and expectations about the piece of writing to be undertaken. Readers as well as writers can decide to continue or give up at this stage, depending on purpose, interest and motivation. Obviously, for the young reader and writer, it is imperative that they are motivated to continue, find the task interesting, are aware of the purpose of this task and, above all, feel successful.

What Readers Do DURING Reading	What Writers Do DURING Writing

The proficient reader is engaged in:
- draft reading
  — *skimming and scanning*
  — *searching for sense*
  — *predicting outcomes*
  — *re-defining and composing meaning*
 	
- re-reading
  — *re-reading parts as purpose is defined, clarified or changed*
  — *taking into account, where appropriate, an audience*
  — *discussing text, making notes*
  — *reading aloud to "hear" message*
- using writer's cues
  — *using punctuation to assist meaning*
  — *using spelling conventions to assist meaning*
	The proficient writer is engaged in:
	- draft writing
	  — *writing notes and ideas*
	  — *searching for a way in, a "lead"*
	  — *selecting outcomes*
	  — *re-reading*
	  — *revising and composing meaning*
	
	- re-writing
	  — *re-writing text as purpose changes or becomes defined, clearer*
	  — *considering readers and the intended message*
	  — *discussing and revising text*
	  — *re-reading to "hear" the message*
	- preparing for readers
	  — *reading to place correct punctuation*
	  — *proof-reading for conventional spelling*
	  — *deciding on appropriate presentation*

Draft reading and writing can be defined as the "refinement of meaning which occurs as readers and writers deal directly with the print on the page" (*Tierney and Pearson* 1983, p. 571). What every reader needs, like every writer, is a first draft—an opportunity to "have a go" at working on the text without fear of being wrong.

A reader opens his or her textbook, magazine or novel; a writer reaches for his or her pen. The reader scans the pages for a place to begin; the writer holds the pen poised. The reader looks over the first few lines of the article or story in search of a sense of what the general scenario is . . . The writer searches for the lead statement or paragraph to the text . . . Once (the scenario is) established the reader proceeds through the text, refining and building upon his or her sense of what is going on; the writer does likewise. (*Tierney and Pearson* 1983, p. 571)

What Readers Do AFTER Reading	What Writers Do AFTER Writing
The proficient reader: • responds in many ways, e.g. talking, doing, writing • reflects upon it • feels success • wants to read again	The proficient writer: • gets response from readers • gives to readers • feels success • wants to write again

The above model is over-generalised but is useful to demonstrate the similarities between the processes of reading and writing. Considering the processes in this way demonstrates the many implications for the teaching of reading and writing.

What also becomes apparent is that neither reader nor writer can exist without a text. Writers must produce them and readers must interpret them and the text always stands between the two— a bridge as well as a barrier:

Text is a two-sided mirror rather than a window, with writers and readers unable to see through to each other but gazing upon reflections of their own minds. (*Frank Smith* 1982, p. 87)

The reader relies on the writer to employ appropriate "conventions".

Conventions of written language

If the reader is to receive the intended message, the writer must follow certain "conventions" (Smith, 1982). The reader relies on the writer to employ appropriate conventions and the writer relies on the reader to expect them. The text thus becomes a bridge between the reader and writer when the writer uses conventions which the reader anticipates and follows. The closer the author's intention is to the reader's expectation, the greater the understanding. When this does not occur we say that the writer is too obtuse, uses over-difficult language, or writes on a subject which doesn't interest us.

These conventions are embedded in the text and aid communication between reader and writer. They are more than the surface features of the text, such as punctuation and spelling. They include all those components which make one piece of text different from another—a novel different from a street directory, a poem different from a recipe. The conventions can be categorised thus:

1. **Presentation and Layout.** Different types of texts are organised and presented according to subject matter and purpose, e.g. a telephone book is not written and organised in the same way as a cookery book, and is therefore read differently.

2. **Register.** Different subject areas, purposes and readers require different forms, styles and "registers" of language, e.g. a novel is written in a different register to a science text book; a letter to a favourite aunt will not be written in the same register as a business letter. Register is the kind of language appropriate for a particular purpose in a particular situation. The register used in any situation is determined by what is actually taking place, who is taking part, and what part the language is playing.

3. **Cohesion.** Different registers bring into play different sets of "cohesive ties". Language in any text, whether spoken or written, is held together by various cohesive ties. Sentences in a paragraph or paragraphs in a text are knitted into a meaningful piece by the cohesive ties. Reference words such as pronouns are good examples of cohesive ties. (For further reading see M. A. K. Halliday and Ruqaiya Hasan, *Cohesion in English*, Longman, 1976; John Chapman, *Reading Development and Cohesion*, Heinemann, 1983.)

4. **Surface Features.** The use of conventional spelling and punctuation also differs according to the subject area, purpose and readers, e.g. an advertiser will alter spelling as an attention-getting gimmick: *Heinz meanz beanz.*

How do we learn these conventions and know when to use them appropriately?

Frank Smith believes that we certainly cannot learn them all through didactic teaching: "What is learned is too intricate and subtle for that, and there is too much of it. There is just not enough time" (Smith 1983, p. 561). It is mainly through *reading* that writers initially learn all the techniques they know. To learn how to write for a newspaper one must read newspapers; to write poetry one must read poetry. Smith says: "Children must read like a writer, in order to learn how to write like a writer" (1983, p. 562).

What does Smith mean by the term "read like a writer"?

When we read like a writer we are consciously aware of the way the author has written the piece. It is rather like "Saturday Social" tennis players watching professionals in action. Because the watchers are tennis players too, they are more capable of appreciating the skill and finer points of style than people who have never played before. The weekend amateur players who are having trouble slicing a backhand stroke know how hard it is and so watch carefully as the experts play. They actively seek to learn from the demonstrations of others and are highly motivated to practise observed techniques. The more skilled the observers, and the more tennis they play, the greater the learning experience is likely to be.

In the same way, learners who regard themselves as writers will read differently from those who do not write. As they read, they will not only appreciate the conventions and elements of style used by other writers but will actively seek to learn from them. Furthermore, comprehension is thereby greatly enhanced. Not only do they read for meaning, they see beyond that and "befriend" the author. It is as if they step into the author's shoes as they read. Frank Smith takes this point further:

> The author becomes an unwitting collaborator. Everything the learner would want to punctuate, the author punctuates. Every nuance of expression, every relevant syntactic device, every turn of phrase, the author and learner write together. Bit by bit, one thing at a time, but enormous amounts of things over the passage of time, the learner learns, through reading like a writer, to write like a writer. (*Smith* 1983, p. 564)

Do readers always read like writers?

Accomplished readers need not read like a writer *every* time they read. It will not occur, Smith suggests, when the attention of readers is "overloaded"; when they have trouble understanding what they are reading; when they are concentrating on getting the facts or concerned with not making mistakes, as in reading aloud; "And it does not occur when we have no expectation of writing the kind of written language we read". (*Smith* 1983, p. 563)

Literature and all other written materials provide a storehouse of demonstrations of written language for us all. Bill Martin Jnr expresses it neatly:

> Each of us has a linguistic storehouse into which we deposit patterns for stories and poems and sentences and words. These patterns enter through the ear (and the eye) and remain available throughout the course of a lifetime for reading and writing and speaking. The good reader is a person who looks at a page of print and begins triggering patterns that have been stored in his linguistic treasury. These patterns range all the way from the plot structure an author has used in the story, to the rhyme scheme that hangs a poem together, to the placement of an adjective in front of a noun as part of the shape of the sentence, to the underlying rhythmical structure in a line of prose or poetry, to the "ed" ending as part of the shape of the word. (*Martin* 1975, p. 16)

Writing, therefore, is never truly individual but results from clever orchestration of many "chunks of meaningful language" taken from countless language situations. These meaningful chunks are stored and used quite unconsciously by writers. Therefore, we need exposure to a wide range of literature and other printed materials in order to build up our linguistic storehouse, so that we in turn can use the language to which we have been exposed. This is the way we learn the language of books, the language of literacy.

Reproduced here is one part of a twelve page story by eight year old Carl, entitled *The Big Bad Wolf*. It demonstrates that he can already use effectively the conventions required for "once upon a time" narratives. He has built up a storehouse of language models from many other "once upon a time" stories he has heard or read. Expressions such as "very, very weary and tired"

6 find the big bad wolf but Denece didnot now that in the dark dark woods theres a dark dark in the dark dark house house was th was the big bad wolf finely Denece gave up

and "in the dark, dark woods there's a dark dark house" have been heard or read previously by Carl. He was, however, not consciously aware of using any language models. When asked how he knew to write those particular phrases, he replied: "They just came out of my head". His teacher had not read *The Dark, Dark Wood* to the children, and his earlier teachers were not aware of having done so either. But Carl had been exposed to it at some time in his life and it had become part of his own storehouse of language upon which he is able to call when writing narratives.

Carl's exposure to *factual* writing has not been so wide, as demonstrated by his next piece in which he has attempted factual writing but in an inappropriate (narrative) register. He has not used the conventions expected by a reader of non-fiction, and

so the piece is difficult to read. His poor use of punctuation adds to the confusion for the reader.

All About Animals
This animal story has lots and lots of diferont speasnies of lots of Animals the first. Animal well sort of a fish but It is a whale and did you know that a whale coms up to the sirfis. to breath now I am going to tell you abuot turtles the turtle can live in water and on land. the giant turtle comes up from the water a lays all most 4000 eggs thats all about the turtle now im going to tell you about wombats the wombat lives in

Carl's teacher, realising the problem, deliberately introduced him to the Macdonald "Starters in Science" series of books, which are written in the factual register. His teacher knew that Carl would be interested in reading them and that they would assist him with his writing. After six weeks, Carl began to use the conventions in his writing which he, as a reader, had come to expect. The result, the second piece, is easier to read and understand. He is beginning to follow the established conventions of factual writing.

Animals are in evry cuntry and in everty sea Some animals are big and some are small and some are tall or some can be short.

The bigest Animals were the Dinursaws Tithose them big animals long long a go that roould the the world The bigest Dinursaw was the Diplodicus

Carl is now beginning to follow the established conventions of factual writing.

All writers, young and old, experience similar problems to Carl when they are required to write in an unfamiliar register. The difference between the experienced adult writer and the beginning young writer is that adults realise that it helps to have models to follow and may consciously read material in a particular register so that they might become familiar with the appropriate conventions for that register. They "read like a writer". However, young readers and writers need help in looking for, identifying and employing conventions used in different registers. By using literature and a variety of other reading materials in a child's environment as models, teachers can help children "read like a writer". Thus may children discover the many conventions and use them accordingly.

How the reading/writing processes assist each other

If the reading and writing processes are closely linked, how does one assist the other? What do we learn about writing when reading, and about reading when writing?

What We Learn **About Writing** While Involved in the Reading Process	What We Learn **About Reading** While Involved in the Writing Process

PRESENTATION AND LAYOUT

The reader learns:
- the way it is done in different sorts of print matter, in which the purpose can be determined by layout, e.g. advertisements
- that symbols and other prosodics are used to add impact and meaning to writing

The writer learns:
- to expect different purposes as indicated by presentation and layout
- to use all the other information on the page, e.g. symbols, pictures

REGISTER

The reader learns:
- that text should follow a logical sequence so that it makes sense
- that different registers follow different sets of conventions
- that there needs to be sufficient information to allow readers to follow what is happening and make predictions about what might be coming
- that there are different registers for different purposes and audiences
- that there are beginnings, endings, sequencing of ideas, events, etc. appropriate to different registers

The writer learns:
- to expect text to follow a predictable sequence in order to make sense
- to appreciate and notice conventions authors use in different registers
- to predict likely outcomes based on information given in the text
- to expect particular registers appropriate to purpose and audience
- to expect certain beginnings, endings, sequencing of ideas, events, etc. according to different registers

COHESION

The reader learns:
- that writers use "cohesive ties" to knit text together so readers can follow it

The writer learns:
- to expect the "cohesive ties" used to knit text together

SURFACE FEATURES

The reader learns:	The writer learns:
• the function of punctuation in text	• to expect punctuation to guide us in our reading
• spelling conventions, i.e. how words *look* in print, e.g.	• word attack skills, i.e. how words can be represented in print, e.g.
— initial letter	— initial sound
— final letter	— final sound
— the shape of the word	— recall what word looks like
— analysing words	— synthesising words
— syllables	— syllabification

Once we understand the writing process and the reading process, and the similarities between them, we are able to see how reading serves writing and how writing serves reading. *We can read without ever having written, but we cannot write without having read.* Writing involves continuous reading and re-reading of what is on the page. We believe that to write effectively we must "learn to read like a writer". To read effectively we must be exposed to a variety of written materials and their conventions.

What then does all this mean for teaching of literacy? It means that we must reconsider many of the current teaching practices being used in reading and writing. Many teachers began this change with the adoption of "process-writing" in their classrooms. Others have been using literature-based or thematic-based reading programs. Still others are teaching "literacy" through a program which involves the integration of components of reading, writing, spelling, handwriting and language study. Their children are given the responsibility to choose the topics they want to write about and the books they want to read. The motivation to read and write is sustained by the sense of ownership the children have in their work.

The classrooms of these teachers are exciting places in which children are learning literacy skills in a meaningful context, with ease and enjoyment beyond our (and their) previous expectations. The purpose of the remainder of this book is to share the exciting experiences of the many teachers who are moving "towards a reading-writing classroom".

PART 2
THEORY INTO
PRACTICE I

Chapter 4
Classroom practice—how?

Implications of this theory for classroom practice

"Where to now?" is the question we need to ask. So far, we have seen how children succeed in learning how to speak, given the seven conditions which Brian Cambourne has described. These conditions are relevant not only for learning to talk but also for learning to read, write, spell or speak a second language. Next we examined the ways in which proficient readers and writers go about their tasks, and we showed how reading assists their writing development and how writing assists their reading development, both being language processes. But what does all this mean for classroom practice?

As a teacher at an in-service course put it: "It all seems so perfectly logical when I'm here. But what do I do in my classroom tomorrow? How do I put the theory into practice? That's the hard part." Well, that is what this book hopes to explain.

In planning to move towards a reading-writing classroom, in which this theory can be translated into practice, teachers need to consider the following five points. Each one depends upon the other, and together can be viewed as a change in emphasis or a re-focusing of ideas rather than something completely new.

1. Time

Every day, adequate time must be provided for the children to practise the processes of reading and writing. They need time to think about, and talk about, their reading and their writing, and need to know that there will be time to continue any unfinished writing or reading task at the next language period. Time should also be allowed for children to hear good models of written language. Teachers will need to re-examine their use of time accordingly, since the amount of available time in a school day is limited, while the demands on it seem limitless.

2. Ownership

The control and responsibility for the writing and the reading should generally be left with the children. In the main, they should be allowed to choose the topics they want to write about and the books they want to read. These choices will stem mainly from their own experiences and interests. Unknown spellings may be "guessed" or "invented" as a piece is written; punctuation, too, is often ignored in the early stages. Similarly, when they encounter unfamiliar words in their reading, children may make reasonable guesses about them, based on their prior knowledge and the context of the piece they are reading. Sometimes an unknown word will be skipped if it does not affect the overall meaning for the reader.

The purpose for the reading and the writing needs to be established for, and if possible with, the children. The young writer decides upon the appropriate register and style of writing according to the purpose of the piece, and its supposed readership. The reader decides what form an appropriate response might take, e.g. to talk, to draw, to write, to act out—or perhaps do nothing at all. Teachers need to provide options for children to respond to reading, and they should value every child's response. Rather than saying: "That's wrong", we need to ask: "What does that mean? Why did you say/write that?" Teachers need to re-examine their teaching strategies and materials and general attitude to the teaching of reading and writing.

3. Process

There should be an emphasis on the processes of both reading and writing evident in teaching practices and in the classroom environment. The writer should be given the opportunity to rehearse, draft, revise and publish the writing instead of being expected to produce a polished piece all at once. Likewise the reader needs opportunity to "draft", read, revise and respond to printed texts instead of being expected to answer questions after a cold, "one-shot" reading. Through the daily allocation of time, the young reader-writer can be supported and guided by the teacher before and during the reading or writing processes as well as after. Equal

emphasis should be placed on each of these learning phases. Too often, in reading, an over-emphasis is placed on what happens during and after the reading whilst very little emphasis is placed on what support might be needed before the reading begins. In writing, the emphasis is too often on the finished product. This "testing syndrome", the over-emphasis on the product, is due to a failure to see both reading and writing as processes.

4. Conference

Brief discussions or "conferences" with an individual child or small group of children may occur before, during or after the reading or writing takes place. This is a valuable use of teaching time, allowing the teacher to provide individualised support and guidance at the child's own point of need.

The conference is a valuable use of teaching time.

5. Resources

Every classroom should contain a wide range of reading materials, including children's literature (fiction, non-fiction, poetry), newspapers, pamphlets, brochures and magazines. This material should be freely available for children to read and also for use as stimulus and models for their own writing. These materials most certainly can include "readers" from reading schemes. Teachers need to examine these materials carefully in light of the purposes for reading, and needs of the children, so that the "readers" are used as a resource, not as the "program". Reference materials such as dictionaries, directories and atlases should also be on hand, as well as a range of paper, cardboard, pens and pencils. All these resources are necessary, and need to be accessible at all times.

Once teachers recognise and accept the importance of these five major considerations, and alter their classroom practices and environment accordingly, they will turn their classroom into dynamic language-learning workshops.

In order to collect data for the writing of this book, we visited several such classrooms in Australia and New Zealand and witnessed many teachers and children in action. For each visit our initial plan was to sit in the background and observe the teachers and children at work. However, because of the very nature of these classrooms, we were soon drawn into the activities going on in them. Children asked for our guidance, shared their work and generally chatted with us. They gave us the impression that "any adult would do" as a helpful learning resource.

After each session in the classroom, we interviewed the teachers in an attempt to gain insight into how they set up and manage their classrooms. The remainder of this chapter is an attempt to share these experiences and insights with you.

Maxine's classroom

Children in New Zealand start school when they turn five; Maxine Murphy is a team teacher, sharing a class of about one hundred of these beginners at the Conifer Grove school in Auckland. These children were a quite average group, from a range of socio-economic and racial backgrounds, even though, from what follows, it might be imagined that they were a select group. The opposite is the case. When I walked into Maxine's room I found it difficult to believe that the children in her class were just five years old. Everyone was working, throughout the entire room. One group was "reading along" at a listening post. Others were cutting out shapes and drawing pictures of characters from a story they had just heard. Another group, sitting on large, soft, cushions, was reading library books in the library corner. Others were doing a sequencing activity which involved reading the pages of a book which the teacher had pulled apart and mounted on separate sheets of cardboard. It was a story they had heard and read with the teacher and now they were placing the pages into a meaningful sequence. Others were reading from a collection of books which the teacher had read to them many times before. Some were writing about a topic of their own choice, while another group was reading home-made "big books" which were copies of stories introduced during a shared book experience. Yet another group was happily reading and singing together, using the overhead projector and transparencies of familiar nursery rhymes and songs. A boy was reading to Maxine and, as she listened, she added to the cumulative records which she kept for each child. A girl was using magnetic letters to make words she knew. Another child was matching captions to a wall story that had been painted the previous day.

Maxine then assembled the children who had been reading in the library corner. She read them a new story, which they discussed. She drew their attention to the word *was*, which was repeated often in that story. It was in this setting that she did most of her direct teaching. At no time did other children interrupt her when she was working with this group. After about ten minutes this group moved to the listening post to "read along" with a recording of the story they had just heard. The children at the listening post had, meanwhile, moved to the library corner.

Maxine walked around the room checking that everyone was coping. She paused to work with a child who had apparently been having difficulties earlier. She then went over to the writer's corner where she read some of the children's stories. She commented to one proud writer: "Gee, that's interesting. You sure know a lot about ducks, Taki."

She spent some time "conferencing" with these eight children before moving off to another group. The children knew to store their drafts in their writing folders unless they wanted them published. Taki decided he wanted his piece published in a book *shaped* like a duck, so he put his draft into a tray marked "For Publishing". Later that day, Maxine would type his story, using conventional spelling and punctuation, while Taki dictated it to her. He would then illustrate his "duck-book" before it would be used in turn as part of the class reading program.

There were no stencils, no workbooks and no drill. During the Language Workshop every child had opportunity to read, write, talk, listen and think. The children in Maxine's class seemed quite capable of finishing one task, leaving it to be checked if necessary, and progressing independently to the next. What might seem to some to have been a chaotic classroom was, in fact, a hive of organised, purposeful learning—and it was just the same on subsequent visits.

Suddenly, a gentle tap on a triangle caused the children to stop exactly where they were, and look toward the teacher, who quietly said: "It's nearly lunch-time children, so begin packing up". Within five minutes, every item of equipment, every book, every piece of work was back in its place and the children were sitting together singing and chanting rhymes. A little girl conducted this session by holding up a chart on which were written the words of the rhymes. She pointed to the words as the others sang and read. Once all the children were settled on the mat Maxine sent them off to lunch.

"How do you do it?" I asked Maxine in amazement. She just laughed self-consciously and said: "Oh, I don't know. I suppose I'm just organized." My questions flowed: "How do the children know what to do? How do they know when to change around? Did you somehow tell them to move? How do they know where everything belongs? How come they don't go to you all the time? What do they do if they need help? When do you check their work? How do you know the activity is right for them? Do you ever teach them all together?"

"Hang on! Hang on!" she said. "One at a time. The children and I spend the first four to six weeks of every year establishing routines. Together we decide where the book boxes should be kept, where the writing corner should be and what should be in it, and so on. Then it is *our* job (not just mine) to make sure everything is in its correct place. Of course we label everything *together* too, so the children can read the labels. I also use symbols besides the labels to help them. I try to make sure there is enough for them to do so they don't need to always consult me. When I introduce new learning centres (places where children do different activities) throughout the year, or something becomes a hassle, we reassess the organisation and try to come up with a solution that suits us all. It's amazing how responsible the children become when they feel that it's *our* classroom, not just mine.

"They are also shown how and where to get the paper, the pencils, their books and so on, and I encourage them to ask one another for help rather than seek permission and guidance from me all the time.

"I prepare a chart for each day's activities. It tells each group the four or five activities I expect them to do that day. In the 45 minute period, they know they can choose to spend as much time as they need at any one activity. Generally, they follow the activities I suggest, but they know that they don't have to do everything if they don't want to.

"It's important, of course, that I know who has

Monkeys	Goldfish	Bears	Cats	Frogs
1. □□□ Stories in order	1. ◌◌	1. ajr match letters	1. Charts ▤	1. Ⓣ
2. O.H.P.	2. Big books	2. ▤	2. Ⓣ	2. Flannel board
3. Charts	3. ▤	3. Ⓣ	3. ▤	3. Magnetic letters
4. ▤ BookBox	4. Ⓣ	4. ABC Library	4. Books	4. Library
5. Ⓣ	5. ◠◠ stories/captions	5. Poem/song cards	5. Library	5. ▤

Maxine's daily activities chart.

done what, so that I can guide the children if they get into a rut. At the end of every Language Workshop I ask the children to indicate which activities they did and I quickly note their names beside the activity. I find that sometimes the children like the security and the freedom of staying with one activity for a while, especially if they are involved in writing an interesting piece. This does not worry me, as long as it doesn't go on for too long. For instance, Taki has been writing that story for the last couple of days. It's finished now, so tomorrow I'll direct him to some reading activities.

"I spend a lot of time planning these activities to ensure that all children are meaningfully occupied when they are not working with me. Most of the evaluation is done while the children are working. I try to make a time for every child at least once a week (apart from the daily group work) during which I update my cumulative records. I don't worry if I don't see every child every day. The children help each other and I know that they are learning. I don't have to witness everything because I can tell they are learning by observing their writing and reading. Through examining their drafts in writing, and informally examining their reading behaviour, I know where they are and what they need next. For instance, I have observed that many children are beginning to hear and use initial consonants and so I can reinforce this both in their reading and their writing."

"What about class work? Do you ever do anything as a whole class?"

"I start every Language Workshop with the whole class together. (You came in just after we'd broken into groups.) We do shared book experience at this time. After reading some rhymes, songs and stories together we either dramatise one, write a group story about something we've done, like our trip to the local shopping centre, or we write an innovation on a known story."

She went on to explain more about shared book experience and how she taught most of the reading skills and strategies through that approach. She also outlined how she used books as models for writing. Together, teacher and children examine spelling strategies and punctuation; thus, many writing skills are also taught in this session. Maxine sums it up: "I see shared book experience as the basis of my whole language program". (For further discussion of shared book experience, see Chapter 7.)

David was working with a small group on the floor. They were working on a draft of a wall story that they had written the day before. It was an innovation on *And the Teacher Got Mad*, one of the "City Kids" (Nelson) series of books written by Lorraine Wilson. This is how their story went:

> Glenn threw sand at the window
> and the teacher got mad.
> Rebecca coloured in with textas
> and the teacher got mad.
> Nick was fighting with Jason
> and the teacher got mad . . .

Their version finished with:

> Belinda left her book at home
> and D.M. went berserk!!

(D.M. are the teacher's initials!)

David's classroom

David Malmgren teaches Grade One at Moonee Ponds West (Vic.). His classroom was very different. There certainly didn't seem to be "a place for everything and everything in its place". In fact it appeared to be quite untidy. Children and books and work and things were everywhere in a very small room. It looked so crowded. But the atmosphere was magic! There was a warmth and a friendliness that made it a lovely place to be in.

When I walked in I was greeted by six-year-old Lana, the class chatterbox, who immediately checked me out and gave me a guided tour. I realised then that there was more organisation to this room than met the eye.

and the teacher got mad

CITY KIDS

Written by
Lorraine Wilson
Illustrated by
Stephen Axelsen

First the children re-read their story and had a good chuckle. Then David covered some of the words with blank pieces of card using "Blu-tack" to allow them to stick but not damage the book. He masked the words *sand* (noun), *texta* (noun), *fighting* (present participle), *her* (pronoun), and *berserk* (adverb). For each word, the children were asked to substitute other words which would fit. Always, David suggested they read the whole sentence again to check that their choice made sense. The discussion that ensued was very impressive indeed. The children demonstrated that they had a thorough understanding of functional grammar, despite the fact that not one of them knew any of the terminology of grammar. They had enormous fun trying to supply substitutes for the final word "berserk" but decided it was the best possible word. Later, the children would draw the appropriate illustrations on large sheets of cardboard. David would add the text, put on a cover, and staple the whole lot together to make it ready for use in class reading.

Whilst this was going on, another group of children was writing and sharing their work with a parent-aide. Two other children were sitting reading library books in an old bathtub filled with cushions. Lana insisted on showing me the many "big books" they had made. One that she was particularly proud of was *The Day Lana Was Away*, which the class had written co-operatively one day when she *was*, in fact, away from school.

Some of the big books were about happenings the class or an individual had experienced. Others were based on highly predictable and repetitive stories, including traditional stories and some from "Story Box" (Rigby Education) and "City Kids" (Nelson) books. All had been illustrated by the children and were magnificently and imaginatively presented, such is the standard of publishing that

---

> The Day Lana was Away
> When Lana was at school it was SO NOISY.
> The teacher was always saying: BE QUIET!
> One day Lana was away. It was...
> so quiet.
> We had show and tell. It was...
> so quiet.
> We had maths. It was...
> so quiet.
> We had games. It was...
> so quiet.
> And we had art and craft. It was...
> so quiet you could hear people pasting!
> On Monday Lana came back to school. It was
> SO NOISY.
> "BE QUIET!" we all yelled.

Text of class-written "big-book".

David sets in his room. Because the layout and presentation and stories are so good, they are enjoyed as much as the professionally produced trade books and are as well read by the children.

When I asked David how he managed his class he said: "It all just seems to happen. One thing just flows out of another. When we start a session I read several books to the class. Then I send one group off to do an activity which would be related to the reading which that group did the previous day. This might be, for instance, drawing the story in picture

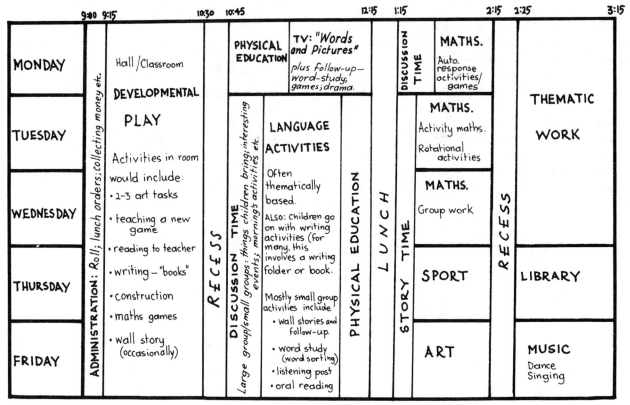

David's time-table.

sequence and writing the story in their own words. Another group goes off to the writing corner. I usually have a parent-aide who helps out there. And I always spend the last part of the session with them working through their writing. The rest of the kids work with me.

"I listen to the kids in order to pick up and build on the funny experiences. *Excuses, Excuses* and *The Day Lana Was Away* came from experiences like this. Sometimes I provide the children with a writing model, or plan an experience. I feel the children in my class need many common experi-ences in English, due to their varied ethnic backgrounds. There is always plenty of time every day for them to read and write what they want to. I use their writing in order to evaluate individual needs. I publish their individual writing too, so the amount of reading material in the room continues to grow. The children love to read each other's books.

"I always treat and teach the children as individuals. Once you know the kids, that's easy. I use lots and lots of literature. I couldn't teach without heaps and heaps of good books. They are my 'text books' and my constant resource."

Bronwen's Learning Space

Bronwen Scarffe teaches Year 1 children at Deer Park North (Vic.). Her classroom was different again. She was in the middle of a theme called "The Entertainers". Everything in the classroom reflected that theme. Apart from the usual library corner, writing corner, listening post and word study area, she had set up the following:

- "Team Two's Theatre Company", a curtained stage which was being used for performances
- a puppet theatre, which was a refrigerator packing-carton, now suitably painted and decorated
- a display of books associated with the theme
- a dress-up box containing hats, scarves, jewellery, shoes, pipes and other props, complete with mirror and make-up
- a shadow-puppet area with an overhead projector and screen
- an art-craft area which contained lots of materials suitable for making props and costumes and puppets of all kinds.

Bronwen began the session with fifteen minutes of uninterrupted sustained silent reading (which she called SQUIRT—Sustained Quiet Reading Time). This was followed by shared book experience in which Bronwen introduced the "blown up" book, *Smarty Pants*, from "Story Box".

After reading the story to the children and discussing what a "smarty pants" was, Bronwen invited the children to "read-along", particularly the refrain "Rum-Tum . . ." She read it to them again and this time the children were asked to mime the various antics that Smarty Pants gets up to. They then made up new actions and Bronwen wrote verses which included these new actions,

following the same pattern. When the children read their verse, they soon realised they needed to alter the final word of the refrain so that it rhymed with their action. For example:

I am a smarty pants,
Rum-tum-tie.
See me reach up
To the sky.

One of the children then noticed that the spelling of *tie* differs from the spelling of *sky*, even though both words rhyme. Bronwen explained that English spelling was often like this and, taking this lead, asked children to supply other words which

I am a smarty pants,
Rum-tum-toe.
Here is a racing car.

From Smarty Pants *(Story Box).*

rhymed. She wrote all the various spellings they volunteered onto a sheet of cardboard. These words would later be categorised and copied onto a large sheet of cardboard to make a "word bank". Other word banks hung all around Bronwen's room; the children were able to refer to them whenever the need arose. This is one of the ways Bronwen teaches spelling and "phonics".

Bronwen's "word-banks".

Bronwen finished off the shared book session by reading aloud C. J. Dennis' poem "The Circus", the children marching around the room in time to the rhythm.

Bronwen's class then divided into several small interest groups. One group was busy re-writing a well-known story as a play. Another was making papier-mache puppets of the characters in a play from a commercially produced book. Another was rehearsing a play which the class had written to perform for younger children in the school. Others were reading books or writing stories of their own

choice. During this time, Bronwen moved from group to group, stopping to assist where necessary.

Noticing that the play-writing group was having difficulty differentiating between direct speech and narrative, Bronwen sent one of the children to find a book which contained a lot of direct speech. She used this text to illustrate the use and function of "talking marks". As the group pored over the book, discussing how to solve their problem, Bronwen moved on to the play-rehearsing group, which needed help. The narrator was reading out the stage-directions as well as the script. Bronwen

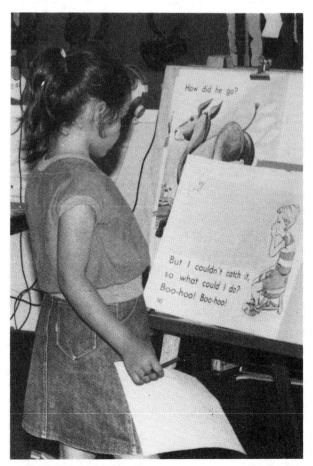

Proficient writers refer to print to learn appropriate conventions.

interrupted to explain that this was inappropriate, pointing out that stage-directions were merely instructions for directors and actors, and not part of the spoken text of the play. Such directions were often set in italics to indicate the difference: "You read that part so that you know what to do. But you don't read it aloud."

Next, Bronwen moved to a section of carpet and sat down. The children who were writing knew that this was a signal for them to come to her to discuss their work, i.e. for a "conference". Two children did this. One had completed his work and was ready to publish; the other was having difficulty. They chatted with Bronwen for a few minutes and then went back to their tables. Bronwen called the other writers over, one by one, to talk with them about their writing, guide them where necessary and suggest what they might do next. She collected two pieces to publish for the children and made a few notes in her record book about the writing progress of these children. The language period ended with a brief sharing time in which one child talked about a book she had just read and another read a story he had been writing and editing over several days.

In response to my question, "How do you manage your classroom?" Bronwen replied: "I plan the whole language theme carefully with the other members of my team, which consists of four other teachers. Although we may follow the theme differently in our classrooms, we always plan it together so that we get everyone's ideas. Firstly, we list the basic beliefs we have about language and language-learning. Then we set out the things we would like to do and how we might do them. Before actually beginning the theme, we set up the physical environment of the classroom to reflect and support the theme. We collect, organise and display relevant resources. The displays and the materials will change as the theme develops. We

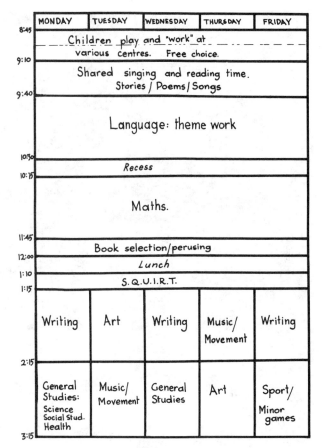

Bronwen's time-table.

list the language skills and objectives we want the children to achieve through this theme and the activities we intend to use to realise these objectives. A flow chart which summarises the theme is drawn up and the evaluation planned."

Bronwen firmly believes that: "The important part of getting started is being prepared".

Robyn Platt's classroom.

Robyn's classroom

The timetable on the door of Robyn Platt's classroom at Grays Point (NSW) reads "Language Workshop—10.00 a.m. to 11.10 a.m. daily". It was 10.30 a.m. when we entered. In the room were thirty children (eight year olds), a parent-aide and Robyn. Everyone was busily reading, writing, talking or listening to someone else. There were no obvious directions being given, there was no group work, yet every child was totally occupied. We observed children as they moved from reading to writing and from writing to reading. The children seemed to know exactly what to do and needed no supervision in going about their work. The parent-aide listened to children reading from their own writing as well as from books. Robyn worked with individual children as they moved through reading or writing activities. She made notes in a folder which she carried with her. It soon became apparent that to give a full account of what was going on in this classroom would entail describing what *every* child was doing. Learning and teaching in this room were truly individualised.

How does it work? Robyn explains:

Any class can work like this, at any level, whether Year 1 or Year 6. It is not easy, and takes time to get things going. The children are all working well now, but it has taken seven weeks for us to get to this stage, and there are still a few routines I need to establish. I believe the time spent is necessary and worthwhile, because now each child can establish his or her own goals and expectations for learning. All of them are working at a higher level of difficulty than I would have set them, and they all succeed because they are confident learners.

So what do I do? Firstly, I outline briefly for myself what I hope to achieve with the children. This outline then helps me decide which routines to establish first.

Preparation

Before the children start school in the first week, I make sure the paper is there, the folders for storing the writing drafts are prepared, the pencils are sharpened and ready in containers and that the library corner has appropriate books, some of which will be in multiple copies. There are a few charts (e.g. an alphabet chart) already on the walls. Charts of words, sentence beginnings and so on will be put up as these are developed from our class activities. In order to be prepared for these occasions I have pieces of cardboard in assorted colours and sizes. Now I'm ready for the children.

WEEK ONE

1. *Shared book experience*

I begin every Language Workshop with shared book experience, using material which has a high degree of predictability in the text. These books are then placed in the class library so that the children can read them during the Language Workshop. (See Chapter 7 for more on shared book experience.)

I also read to the children every afternoon for fifteen minutes. I might choose short picture-story books which I can read in one sitting, or novels which I read in serial form. We always spend a few minutes discussing what the author has written and how the author has made the story funny, sad, interesting, etc. Sometimes I will copy out particular words or phrases which the author has used and which are of special interest to the children. It is with this routine that I begin the whole program.

2. *Discovering how well the children can write*

To establish "where the children are at", I ask them to write something for me on a topic of their own choice. They may take several days to complete this task or may write several pieces during the week. I collect these first drafts and carefully examine each one. I attach each child's writing to a sheet of foolscap paper and underneath I record all the things the child can already do in written language, such as the spelling strategies being used, the quality of handwriting, etc.

I find it far more useful to note what the children can do rather than what they cannot do. This provides me with a good starting point because it shows "where the children are at" and tells me what I need to do next. This page becomes the first in an on-going record which I keep for each child in a special folder. I add to this record regularly throughout the term and year.

3. *Daily writing*

I introduce the concept of daily writing. During the Language Workshop we discuss routines, and

concepts such as drafts, invented spelling, revising, editing, proof-reading and publishing. I introduce the folders in which the children's writing will be stored. We discuss the many different things they could write about. As many of the children have had the opportunity to write daily the previous year, this is not new to them.

We also begin daily journal writing. The children write daily for a few minutes in a journal which they share with me. For the first few weeks, I respond in writing to every entry with a comment or a question about the content of their writing. Sometimes I ask for more information. Through my contribution I am able to demonstrate any spelling, acceptable grammar and punctuation which I might have noticed were unconventionally used in their pieces. They love to read my comments at the bottom of their work and even the most reluctant writer begins to enjoy adding to the daily journal.

I had no intention of keeping this going forever, because it is too time-consuming. However, in the early days I found that it motivated the children to write and to read and gave me the opportunity to get to know individual children and their interests. We do keep the journal going however, spending a few minutes writing each day, usually during the Language Workshop. I only read what they write if they really want me to. I never correct or edit this writing. The aim of the exercise is to give children an opportunity to attempt personal writing and to sort out their thinking.

4. *Handwriting*

I also introduce handwriting cards. We do the first one as a whole class so that I can go through the routine with them. I prepare thirty cards with the handwriting style they are expected to use. I write a few lines from poems, jingles and tongue-

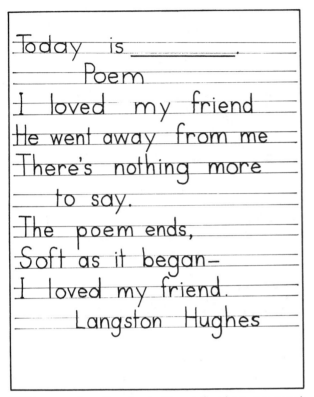

Children copy from these handwriting cards at least once a week in Robyn's classroom.

twisters on each card. I discuss what the children should do with these cards. They are expected to spend some time each week copying, in their best handwriting, the material from one of the cards into a handwriting book. We discuss how to hold a pencil without tension, how to sit so the hand can write without getting tired. We also discuss why it is important to concentrate occasionally on the formation of letters. The children know they need do only one of these cards each week, during the Language Workshop. Most choose to do it early in the week. They leave their books on my table for

my comments. During the first few weeks I examine the handwriting carefully in order to see how I can best assist those children who need help with letter formation and style.

5. Reading at home

We begin our "reading at home" program. The children choose a book to take home each night to read, and may keep the same book for as long as they need it. I don't expect parents to mark cards but I ask them to provide some supportive time for the child to read.

Once these routines have been introduced I continue to remind the children of the "ground rules". Often in these first weeks we will all come together to discuss how things are going, and may alter certain things if they are not working.

WEEK TWO

1. Consolidating the routines

I concentrate on establishing the routines introduced for reading aloud to the children, daily writing, journal writing, handwriting cards and the home reading program. I go very slowly, reminding them of the rules of operation so that they know what is expected of them. The routines we establish are important and need to work smoothly if chaos is to be avoided, although the approach is flexible enough to allow them to be changed whenever necessary. I believe it is imperative that each child knows exactly what to do during the Language Workshop. I have no groups. Children work individually, choosing whatever activity they wish. They know they can work and talk together—and often do—seeking advice and support from each other rather than from me. They do need time and encouragement to get used to the idea of being able to choose what they want to do first during each session—to read, write, or do a handwriting card.

2. Discovering how well the children can read

During this second week I listen to each child reading. Just as I noted all the writing skills the children had demonstrated they knew, I do the same for reading. Each child comes to me during this week and reads a book, or part of a book, chosen from the class library. I keep a record book for each child, in which I make comments on book choice, reading strategies and skills, and attitude to books.

3. Daily reading

We begin our daily reading routine. We have the class library and the Ashton Core Library from which the children may choose any book they want to read. They have an exercise book in which they record the title of each book read, the date begun, and date completed. This record is for me, their parents and themselves and they need to understand the purpose of keeping such information.

When they have finished reading a book they may choose a variety of things to do. The Ashton Core Library has some activity cards which the children enjoy—especially the practical ideas. I have made cards on which I have listed general activities appropriate for the other books. The children don't have to use these cards, but most do. Sometimes they may read several books, then decide to do some appropriate follow-up activities, such as:

- painting a picture of any of the characters or part of the story
- making a model of the story-setting
- making puppets and turning the story into a play
- retelling the story onto a "scroll television"
- drawing the story in cartoon form
- making something from the story from the craft box
- talking to me or the parent-aide about the book
- any other activity they can think of doing

If children tend to stick to the same activity or do no follow-up activity at all, I discuss this and encourage them (and occasionally direct them) to attempt something different.

4. Parent assistance

Towards the end of the second week I send a letter to parents, requesting assistance in the classroom. From the start of the third week, parents help in all sorts of areas, e.g. craft, art, music, publishing children's writing and listening to children read. I bring together those who are prepared to help in this way; we discuss their roles and how they should respond to the children's work. We arrange a roster to ensure that I have a parent-aide in the Language Workshop each day. Parents help out at other times with music, craft and physical education.

WEEK THREE

1. Listening

I now introduce the eight-headphone listening post, which is permanently set up in one corner. I have made my own tape-recordings of readings from many books; each tape-recording is housed in a plastic bag, along with eight copies of the particular book. The children are thus able to listen to the story and to "read along" with me. Children have to "sign up" for this session—they enter their names on a special card if they want to listen to the tape on a particular day. This record works for me too, because it lets me ensure that everyone hears the story. The same tape stays in the recorder for a week; thus each child has ample opportunity to hear it. Some will listen and "read along" several times in the week. These children, I find, are usually the less confident readers, for whom the recording provides welcome support. These children will often choose to borrow the particular book they have been hearing as their "take home" book during the next week.

2. Conferences

I begin "conferences" with children, not just about their writing but also about their reading. After each of these sessions I add notes to my on-going records, and date them.

3. Parent-aides and reading

The parent-aides begin assisting by listening to children read. They know that their role is to encourage children to read for meaning and to attempt unknown words; if necessary the parent will identify unknown words for them. The emphasis is on enjoyment. So that I know what has been read in each session, the children are supplied with a large book-mark which has room for parent-aides to note the title of the book, the part read and the date. Parent-aides are not asked to make any qualitative judgements about the child's reading. Any visiting adult is likely to be viewed as another

Parent aides encourage children to read for meaning.

resource by the children, who enjoy sharing their reading and writing with a wide variety of people.

WEEK FOUR

This week we spend consolidating our program and sorting out any problems. During the Language Workshop, children may read, write, do journal entries, listen to a story or do a handwriting card. I introduce separate cards for all children so that they may keep individual records of what has to be done during the week. These cards also help me to know what each child is doing. At other times of the day, children have fifteen minutes of silent reading and fifteen minutes of being read to.

Name:												
Day	Writing				Reading			Hand-writing card	Listening tape story	Word study guess-book sheet	Other work
	Draft	Journal	Letter	Editing	Library	Core	With an adult				
Monday											
Tuesday											
Wednesday											
Thursday											
Friday											
Monday											
Tuesday											
Wednesday											
Thursday											
Friday											

Robyn's children keep individual records of work.

WEEK FIVE

1. The "guess book" as an aid to spelling

I introduce children to the concept of the "guess book". I cut a normal exercise book in half and write on the cover, for example, "Nicole's Guess Book". (I deliberately use the possessive form so that children can use it as a model.) The "guess book" is an important part of the spelling program. Children are allowed (and encouraged) to invent their own spelling in draft writing, but spelling becomes a teaching point when a piece is being prepared for publication. My first response is always about the message in the child's writing. Once that is sorted out I then ask the child to find four or five words which might have been written in non-conventional spelling (i.e. spelling known to have been "made up"). The child copies these words into the "guess book". Each word is written several ways before the child decides which spelling is the conventional one, or nearest to it. The child then refers to the dictionary or any other reference he or she thinks might contain the word. Children may work co-operatively with others on these words, and often do.

When a child is fairly sure of the conventional spelling for the particular words, a check is made with the parent-aide or myself before they are written into the child's own story. I write the words into the *Class Dictionary* and the child writes each word onto a card to be stored alphabetically in our class "word box". All children know that they should refer to words listed in the *Class Dictionary* to check their own spelling before bringing any writing to me or the parent-aide.

2. Class conference

During the last part of our Language Workshop I bring the children together to discuss things they were doing during the session. Some will share the books they've read and the results of the follow-up activity. Many like to discuss the words they have learned to spell and, naturally, will spell them for the benefit of other children. This leads us into some very interesting discussions about words themselves.

3. Books as models for writing

Although I will have been reading books to the children daily since the first week, I now begin to use many of the books as models of good writing. We examine interesting phrases and words, we notice how the author begins the story, and the punctuation and the spelling used. The children may decide to use these books as models for their own writing. I use some time at the beginning of the Language Workshop for this type of activity, which helps to increase the children's awareness of how other writers write. For instance, after using John Burningham's book *Would You Rather?* we decided to make our own book like it. Several children then proceeded to write their own variations on the comic choices presented in the text of that book. All the books which we use in this way, as well as the children's own published books, are put in the class library. They are used during the Language Workshop either as reading material or as a reference source of ideas for further writing.

WEEK SIX

In this week we begin our class "post boxes". Every child has a "private box" which is simply a milk carton cut and pasted into an oblong shape with a section of the front cut to form a flap. Each box is covered in Contact adhesive film (parents do this), attached to cardboard and then pinned up on the wall. Children then write letters to each other and place them in the appropriate box. The few rules associated with letters are as follows:

- They must be neatly written.
- They must be signed.
- They must be the sort of letter which the writer would like to receive.
- They must be responded to.

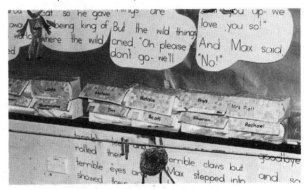

Class post boxes made from milk cartons.

WEEK SEVEN

By this stage my daily time-table is established, the language program is working well, and the children have become used to the procedure. Within the apparent freedom are very strict routines to which the children must adhere. Also built into the program are checks and systems for evaluation. I continually add information to my on-going records. Every six weeks I evaluate the children's progress more formally. I begin by re-reading my informal notes. Next I collect the most current pieces of writing and compare them with earlier samples, noting whatever progress has been made. With this information in mind, I write a summative report which I place in the *Record Book*. I also listen to each child read, before making a more formal assessment, noting the skills the child is now using in reading. As with writing, I look over my informal records and note improvements. When I put all this information together I have a very comprehensive evaluation of each child's progress.

Of course, much reading and writing occurs dur-ing other curriculum areas as well. It is in these areas that I can expose the children to different "registers" of language. This happened, for instance, in Science when we were observing plant growth. The children kept daily diaries, noting the changes in the different plants each day. Finally, in pairs, they wrote a report about what had happened. Similarly, in Social Studies, after discussing television, children had to make up interview questions which would elicit data about which television stations people watch, and their reasons for doing so. As a carry-over, the children will often choose to write about these things during the Language Workshop session.

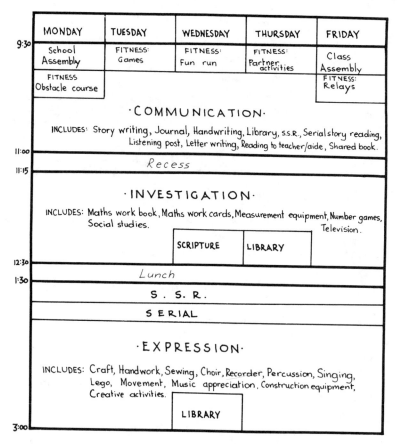

	MONDAY	TUESDAY	WEDNESDAY	THURSDAY	FRIDAY
9:30	School Assembly	FITNESS: Games	FITNESS: Fun run	FITNESS: Partner activities	Class Assembly
	FITNESS: Obstacle course				FITNESS: Relays

·COMMUNICATION·

INCLUDES: Story writing, Journal, Handwriting, Library, s.s.r., Serial story reading, Listening post, Letter writing, Reading to teacher/aide, Shared book.

11:00

11:15 — *Recess*

·INVESTIGATION·

INCLUDES: Maths work book, Maths work cards, Measurement equipment, Number games, Social studies. Television.

SCRIPTURE	LIBRARY

12:30

1:30 — *Lunch*

S. S. R.

SERIAL

·EXPRESSION·

INCLUDES: Craft, Handwork, Sewing, Choir, Recorder, Percussion, Singing, Lego, Movement, Music appreciation, Construction equipment, Creative activities.

LIBRARY

3:00

Robyn's time-table.

Different teachers, common characteristics

What do these teachers have in common? Despite the obvious differences in personality, style of teaching, age-level of class, locality of school, use of resources, etc. all of these teachers manage successful reading-writing classrooms. We have noticed that these teachers have certain characteristics in common and that these largely explain why their classrooms are so effective as learning environments. We identify them as follows:

1. *They know their children*—their interests, likes and dislikes, backgrounds, and idiosyncracies. This assists them in deciding the sorts of materials to present to individual children; how to form groups for different activities and purposes; how to cope with discipline within the classroom; how to have appropriate expectations for each child, and how to provide guidance and support for each child as the need arises.

2. *They know the resources* available with the school and the community. They use them selectively and as an aid to their program rather than as the basis of the program. They rule the resources, not the other way around. They also know what is between the covers of the books they present to the children.

3. *They plan a general program for the whole class, with clear long-term goals.* These goals are based on what the teachers believe about how children learn language. Within that plan, they program specific activities and content to meet the needs of the individuals within their class.

4. *They continuously evaluate* the children's progress, and their own performance, in order to plan further relevant activities. This evaluation takes place while listening and watching the children as they go about their daily activities. Brief anecdotal records are built up over the entire year, entries being made as indications of growth become evident. From time to time, each child is taken aside and his or her reading and writing behaviour is observed closely.

5. *They are organised, yet flexible.* In each classroom there is an area where the whole class can work together. There are also places where individual children and small groups can work. The groupings are kept flexible to avoid labelling, which can be harmful. These teachers also believe that children who have mastered a particular skill will make good teachers for those children who are still in the process of mastering that skill.

6. *They are calmly confident* because they know why they are doing what they are doing. All read widely, attend in-service courses and reflect upon their own practices often. They are prepared to change but they choose selectively from new trends and ideas.

7. *They are aware of the role that language plays* in all areas of the curriculum. Therefore they take advantage of and value the language occurring in all subject areas.

8. *They give children many opportunities to read, write, talk and listen* in a meaningful context. Their children are given opportunities to think about their options and make decisions about their own learning.

9. *They allot **time** wisely.* In their planning they allow time for:

- demonstrating and providing good reading and writing models
- extended periods, each day, during which children may read and write about topics of their own choosing

- responding through art, craft, drama, music, writing, movement, talking and other expressive activities
- sharing, with each contribution being valued; children's stories are read, comments are sought and discussion flows freely
- group interaction, in which children are free to learn from each other.

10. *They allow time for* **teaching**. This may involve the whole class, while at other times it may involve "conferences" with individuals and small groups. Always, the teaching points emerge from the children's needs. And they treat one thing at a time, knowing that learning is a gradual, on-going process. The way time is allocated changes from day to day, from class to class. It is rather like the technique of marbling, in art, in which the artist drops certain quantities of oil-based paint into a tray of water and then drops a clean sheet of paper on the top of the water. Every pattern which emerges is different.

11. *They establish rules of operation* and routines with the children — and then expect them to be followed. This frees them to teach groups and individuals, knowing that the rest of the class can, and will, be working productively.

12. *They actively discourage competition* between the children. They award no marks, no gold stars, and no house points. Conversely, they actively encourage co-operation and peer tutoring.

13. *They surround their children with print.* Their classrooms are filled with models of good reading and writing. Children's work adorns the room and is changed often.

14. *They understand the difference between teaching and learning.* They know that their most important role is to create a stimulating learning environment.

15. *They internalise the theory.* They know how children learn language, what the reading process is, what the writing process is and how reading serves writing, and writing serves reading. They know that children must learn to "read like a writer" for them to develop as writers.

16. *They have flexible attitudes towards grouping.* Although they divide their classes into functional groups, they have no fixed bases for forming such groups. Some might be formed on the basis of interest, need or ability, while others might have no common basis at all. The important thing is that they are flexible.

17. *They treat children with respect,* valuing their opinions, decisions and interests. They encourage them to be responsible for their own decisions and interests. They encourage them to be responsible for their own learning and behaviour. They talk to them as people, not as "little children". They also *earn* the respect of the children, rather than demand it.

PART 3
THEORY INTO PRACTICE II

Classroom practice: what?

Children must read like a writer, in order to learn how to write like a writer. Frank Smith.

Within a theoretical framework, we have already (Chapter 3) discussed the implications of Frank Smith's statement about the inter-relatedness of reading and writing. The question now arises as to *how* we teach children to "read like a writer". It is this question we now wish to address as we get down to practicalities.

We do not intend to discuss *all* the good methods currently being used by teachers as they help children to read and write. Rather, we wish to describe some particularly useful strategies which fall into three main categories, and which commonly occur in successful reading-writing classrooms.

So what should we be doing in our classrooms? Firstly, we must do as Brian Cambourne suggests and *"immerse" children in a great deal of printed material*. We need to give children time and opportunities to see and hear good models of written language, thus providing them with countless demonstrations of how written language is used in functional and meaningful ways.

Secondly, we must *demonstrate uses for writing* with, and in front of children. We need to provide children with time and opportunities for them to write for a variety of purposes, and for a range of audiences.

Thirdly, we must *help children to make the links between reading and writing*. Once they perceive themselves as readers and writers, we need to provide opportunities for them to learn how to "read like a writer".

We will now look at ways in which teachers are putting these three major requirements into action in their own dynamic reading-writing classrooms.

Chapter 5
Immersing children in print

Reading to children

The stories teachers read to children need to be chosen carefully. It is not good enough to grab any book from the library shelf without having thought about *what* is to be read to the children and *why*. It is imperative to be thoroughly familiar with the book *through having read it beforehand*. In this way we can select the right material to suit our own needs as well as the children's, and will be able to present it in the best possible way. The most successful books will be those which we, ourselves, enjoy.

Wise selection will enable time to prepare for issues which could arise and to plan appropriate discussion or follow-up work. Social issues which might arise include sexism, racism, feminism, conservation, and the plight of the disabled and other disadvantaged groups, etc.

We need to read not only stories but a variety of non-fiction as well. Children need to be introduced to different "registers" of written language by first hearing samples. This enables them to cope with the conventions of different registers more easily than if they were left to read them alone. For instance, in Science, the concept-loading and idea

density is extremely high. There is no predictable story line. Facts are given in a logical sequence. There is a high frequency of connectives such as *firstly, therefore, consequently* and *in conclusion,* which children need to understand in order to gain meaning from such passages.

Children need to hear a wide range of registers of written language before we can expect them to *read* a wide range of registers. Therefore we need to read *to* them as well as providing them with opportunities to read. This is necessary for children at all levels of the primary school.

> Esthetic response can only be nurtured. It cannot be taught. By wide and continuing exposure to stories, poems, art, photos and language that possess some pretension to taste, children will begin to know what they do and do not like . . . Be assured those pleasurable times of the day when you read aloud to children are all part of a program in literary and esthetic appreciation, as well as part of the reading program. (*Bill Martin* 1975, p. 117.)

Balancing the reading diet

Teachers should not only read to children from a range of material but should provide an equally wide range for the children's own reading. But it is not enough merely to provide this material. The well-read teacher provides constant guidance for the children by helping them select material appropriate to their interests, abilities and needs.

At Sackville Street Public School (NSW) Rob Hughes tries to ensure that the children in his Year 6 class vary their reading diets. He encourages them to keep a record of books read, under categories such as realistic fiction, science fiction, historical fiction, family stories, humour, fantasy, non-fiction and traditional (e.g. myths, legends). He checks these records regularly and suggests alternative authors, titles and types of reading for children who seem to be limiting their range of reading matter and who should perhaps be experiencing greater variety.

Children making judgements

Viv Nicoll
Macarthur Institute of Higher Education (NSW)

LOW	MID	HIGH

Value line.

I use "value lines" for helping my children to make value judgements about the stories they've read or heard. A value line ranges from a low rating at one end to a high rating at the other. Firstly, I ask the children to list a few of the stories or poems that they have been reading, or have been read to them. Then I ask them to place their opinion of each story somewhere along their personal "value line".

It is important that the children understand that they rate each story in relation to all other stories they have heard or read. That means that, in any one day, all the stories will not necessarily be spread evenly along the line. Once children have made their own personal value judgements, they are ready to meet in small groups to discuss their ratings. This is the part of the activity the children like best. They love to argue and defend their ratings, particularly when someone disagrees strongly with them. Of course, there is no "correct" rating, and they soon realise the subjective nature of most responses to literature. They also learn that it is acceptable to dislike a book which others like, and vice-versa.

These Year 6 girls enjoy opportunities for silent reading.

Uninterrupted Sustained Silent Reading (USSR) or Drop Everything and Read (DEAR)

This is a daily time during which everyone, including the teacher, reads silently for a given period. Children can choose to read anything they wish. It works well at all levels and children love it. Sloane and Latham (1981, p. 32) outline this strategy very clearly. They suggest the following basic steps:

1. Ensure that each child has selected a book to read.
2. Have the children seated at cleared desks from where they have an unobstructed view of the teacher and the teacher can see them.
3. Rehearse the rules for USSR with the children:
   - no interruptions,
   - no changing of books,
   - every child must read silently,
   - teacher must read silently.
4. A timer (e.g. a cooking timer, a digital watch with alarm) is started; everyone, including the teacher, begins reading. The timer is set for an amount of time the children are capable of

sustaining. This may only be three or four minutes at first.

5. Silent reading is continued until the timer rings. At the ringing of the timer, the teacher warmly and enthusiastically congratulates the children by saying: "Good, well done, you've been reading for x minutes. Carry on."
6. Silent reading continues until there are signs of interruption. When this happens, conclude the session quickly by saying: "Thank you, everyone. Books away." Record the time, but don't tell the children. Build the initial time up slowly each day until the children can read for 20-30 minutes without interruption. When this happens you will be able to omit step 5.
7. It is essential to have another task ready as a follow-up. This task must not be related to reading, and definitely not related to anything the child has just read. Children need to feel that the session is for them to enjoy, without feeling they will have to do something about it when they've finished. Sometimes, children will want to discuss their books. This should be done informally.

Old bathtubs have their uses.

The reading conference

The "conference" is recognised as a vital teaching technique in writing. Only recently have teachers begun to recognise its value in reading. Marcia Saunders uses reading conferences with her Year 5 children for many reasons. Her reading program is truly individualised; children choose their own reading materials from the variety displayed in the room. Marcia selects materials carefully to suit the children's reading levels and their reading interests. She has a reading conference with each child at least once a week. During this time she is able to assess such things as levels of reading comprehension and ability to read critically, as well as capacity to form opinions about what has been read. The conference also allows her to ascertain a child's reading needs and interests, and attitudes to reading in general.

Marcia Saunders
Moonee Ponds West Primary School (Vic.)

In our reading time the children know they can browse through the reading materials and select either a book (child-written or otherwise), a magazine or newspaper. They can sit where they like to read, and can stop to discuss their reading with a friend for short periods. Whilst they are reading, I sit on my chair with my note book and talk with children individually in a "reading conference" — a most valuable and satisfying teaching technique. I find out all sorts of things about the children's reading interests and it provides me with a marvellous opportunity to teach each child at the point of need. I can also assess each child's reading during this time. Therefore it is important for me to keep notes on each conference. These informal records become the basis for my evaluation of each child in reading. When I began, I followed the steps outlined by Don Holdaway (1972, p. 55):

1. **Rapport.** Make sure the child is at ease by making some friendly welcoming comment.
2. **Sharing.** Listen as the child tells something about his or her response to the book that is being read. Discuss any related activity he or she may be pursuing. (I try to have read all the materials available to the children so that I know what questions to ask.)
3. **Question.** Ask one or two searching questions concerning the theme of the book, the author's message or point of view, the characters or the setting.
4. **Oral Reading.** Listen to the child read a short part of the piece which he or she has chosen to share.
5. **Record.** Check the child's reading behaviour and make appropriate entries in files about the progress, interest and problems.
6. **Encourage and Guide.** Discuss plans for future reading. Offer suggestions about selection of other books by the same author or around the same theme.

As well as the individual conference, I often organise a group conference with those children who demonstrate they need help in a particular area. I also organise activities such as "cloze", sequencing, etc. to give certain children practice in particular skills of reading.

Since we began this program I have been thrilled with the children's progress in reading and their more positive attitude towards it.

Asking appropriate questions about books read

If the teacher has read the same book as the child, the conference may stimulate discussion and sharing of information. However, if the teacher has not read the book it is more difficult to generate interesting dialogue. Faced with this problem, Sue Hill and the students from South Australia CAE (Magill Campus) devised sets of general questions which a teacher could ask about particular groups of stories. As fantasy, mystery, historical fiction, etc. have particular characteristics, it was possible to devise questions which are generally applicable to most stories within each category. They suggest that these questions could be displayed in the classroom so that children may use them when responding to each other, or when responding in writing, art and craft work, or drama. They will also help the children decide to which category the book they are reading belongs.

Once the children become familiar with the questions they may wish to add more or to create new categories.

A WAY OF TALKING ABOUT BOOKS, USING GENERIC QUESTIONS
Sue Hill and students
South Australian C.A.E. (Magill Campus)

FANTASY STORIES
Is the world in which the story is set similar to our world?
What are the differences?
What special traits or powers do the characters have that we do not?
Do the characters possess these powers at the beginning of the story? If not, how do they discover them?
Are there two opposing forces in the story? If so, what are they?
What are the problems faced by the main characters? How do they solve these problems?
How has the author made the story believable?
If you had been part of the story, how might you have used your one special power to resolve the conflict?
Did you enjoy this fantasy?

MYSTERY STORIES
What was the actual mystery or crime in the novel?
Could you identify with any of the characters in the book?
Was there a motive for the mystery or crime? If so, what was the motive and which characters stood to benefit?
Was the setting in the novel crucial to the mystery? If so, in what way?
What clues did the author give you to help solve the mystery?
Did the author do anything to throw you off the track?
How was the mystery solved, and by whom?
Were you satisfied with the ending? Please explain your answer.
Do you think the events in the book were realistic? Could such things really happen?
Do you think you could plan your own mystery story, similar to the one in the book?
Did you solve the mystery before it was solved in the story? How did you do it?
Were there questions still unanswered at the end of the story?
How did the author build up suspense in the story?

SCHOOL STORIES
Do you ever feel like any of the children in this story?
In what ways is your school life like that in the book?
What do you notice about the groups of friends in your school and in the school in the book?
What different sorts of things do children learn in school and out of school?
Which children in the book enjoy school the most? Why do you think this is so?
How believable is school life in the story, e.g. are the teachers really like that?
Was there a conflict in this story? If so, between whom and why?

FAMILY STORIES
Who are the main characters in the story?
What problems do these characters face and how do they solve them?
What is your favourite moment in the story?
How and why is the life of this family similar or different to your own family life? Give your reasons.
Is there anyone in this family who is a bit like you? Why?

BIOGRAPHY

Who is the main character of the novel? What sort of person is s/he? Is s/he the author?

Where, and in what period of time, is the novel set? Which part of the main character's life is the novel about?

What were some of the main events in the life of the main character?

In what way did the main events affect him or her?

To what extent was the author in control of these events?

Try to place yourself in the character's position. Would you have reacted in the same way to particular events, or would you do things differently? Why?

If given the chance to write your own life story, what things would you tell? How would you tell your story?

ADVENTURE STORIES

Is there a crime or wrong-doing that starts the actions of the book? Who does it?

Is their one main character in the story?

Why is this person the main character?

What sorts of problems occur? How do the characters solve them?

Where and when does the adventure happen?

Are there any animals in the story? Are they important in the adventure? How?

Do adults have an important part? What role do adults play?

Does anyone get punished or caught for something he or she has done wrong? How does this happen?

Does the adventure turn out well in the end?

Did the adventure end the way you expected?

Would you like to have an adventure like the one in the story?

Using the tape-recorder

Stephen Chinnock
Wilkins Public School (NSW)

The tape-recorder is seen as "the other teacher" in my infants classroom when it comes to reading. We use the tape-recorder with the listening post (which has eight headphones) or with just one head-phone. I have prepared many tapes by reading whole stories, poems and extracts from stories recently introduced into the library. Non-fictional material is also used. I have had parents-aides help by either reading books or narrating stories in the several ethnic languages represented in our classroom. All these tapes are clearly marked and stored near the machine so that children may freely choose which ones they would like to listen to.

As well, the children themselves record their own favourite stories and poems. They spend time practising a favourite piece from the book they've just read. Sometimes they do this quite alone, but they may ask a friend to help if necessary. They read and re-read until they are happy with what they read on the tape-recorder. Because they are very particular with expression, they become acutely aware of punctuation. They often use sound effects as well. The result is usually a highly polished production. This cassette is then marked and added to the class "story bank". This "story bank" encourages children to read stories which others have obviously enjoyed. Our tape-recorder is a great friend to have in the classroom.

"Skinny books"

Dulcie Patullo and Joy Stacey
Language Consultants (Queensland)

This strategy is useful with children of all reading levels in middle and upper primary classrooms. "Skinny books" are simply the separate chapters of books which have been pulled apart and made into several smaller sections. Many children find the step between picture-story books and novels to be intimidating, due to the greatly increased amount of text and the lack of pictures. "Skinny books" help them to make that step. The proficient reader may move on to other titles by the same author. The less proficient readers will need more time and support from the teacher, but the important thing is for them to feel that they, too, have read and actually finished a "novel", even though it may only have been part of a longer work.

In the following example of text-sharing we use *Pippi Longstocking* (Puffin), a popular book written by Swedish author Astrid Lindgren. It is ideal for middle primary classes, especially since each chapter is more or less a self-contained story. For the same reason, *My Naughty Little Sister* (Puffin), by Dorothy Edwards, is a good novel for younger children, whereas *Sun on the Stubble* (Rigby), by Colin Thiele, is better for older children.

Using *Pippi Longstocking* to make "skinny books"
Preparation
1. At least two copies of the book are needed, one to keep intact to read to the children and the other to make into separate "skinny books". Pull the chapters apart. Where a page is shared by two chapters you will need to photocopy one side. (This amount is within copyright laws.) Make cardboard covers for each "skinny book", illustrate and label them.
2. Gather together suitable dressing-up clothes, e.g. large men's boots; brown and black stockings; a wig made out of orange crepe paper or wool.
3. Read the ninth chapter of *Pippi Longstocking* onto audio-cassette.

Method
1. On consecutive days, read the first two chapters of the book.
2. After each reading, discuss what is revealed of Pippi as a character, e.g. she is an orphan, is

unusually strong, has a curious appearance and tells "tall" tales.
3. Introduce the "skinny books". Continue to read one a day to the children, particularly to groups which may need extra support.
4. Introduce the dressing-up box to the children and encourage them to dramatise what they've read, using costumes.
5. Introduce the other *Pippi* titles and other books by Astrid Lindgren. Encourage children to read these, and give them opportunities to discuss them.

6. Use some specific activities based on the book:
    (a) Illustrate parts of the story.
    (b) Collect words or phrases which describe the characters.
    (c) "Cloze" activities.
    (d) Children read the "skinny books" to younger children.
    (e) Dramatise parts of the story.
    (f) Retell parts of the story.
    (g) Invent some "tall stories".
    (h) Construct a literary sociogram. This activity helps the children gain insights into an episode (such as that of the ninth chapter) and a better understanding of relationships between characters. We found that children love this activity, which is most successful when all children have read the particular episode or chapter for themselves, or have heard a recording of it on audio-cassette.

    Ask: Who is the most important person in the story?

    Do: Write Pippi's name or draw a picture of her on the centre of the board.

    Ask: Who else is in the story?

    Do: Place other characters around the main character.

    Ask: How does each character feel about Pippi, and how does she feel about them?

    Do: Draw an arrow from Pippi to the first character. Write the children's responses beside it. Draw an arrow in the opposite direction from that character to Pippi. Beside it, write how that person feels about Pippi.

  Repeat this for each character. Where there is any disagreement on a point, ask children to refer to the text to justify their ideas.

We found that using a text-sharing approach such as this helps children to comprehend written language which is at a higher level than they may be able to manage independently. It introduces children into the novel form of literature, thus widening their reading horizons.

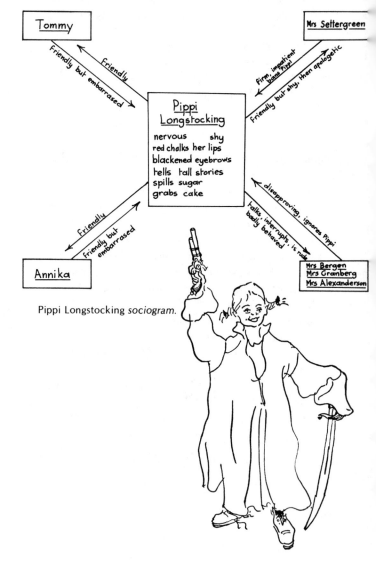

Pippi Longstocking *sociogram.*

Using picture-story books

Denise Ryan
Walters Road Public School (NSW)

There are picture-story books for young children but there are many which are ideal for sharing with older children. Picture-story book texts are usually short and can easily be read in one session. Picture-story books are often beautiful demonstrations of how art and written language may be perfectly combined to convey ideas. I find that my Year 5 children enjoy the whole range of picture-story books once we've begun to look at them in this light. For instance, we began by reading all of Charles Keeping's picture-story books, which are ideally suited to older children, since they examine some very sensitive issues, such as loneliness and death. Once we'd worked through these, we then examined Brian Wildsmith's picture books. Although these are generally used and appreciated by a younger audience, my class loved them, since they were looking at them from a different perspective. They began to bring library books into the classroom. We'd read them and discuss such things as the techniques the author and illustrator have used in combining art and text to convey meaning. These examples may be used as models for the children's own writing later on.

See *Bibliography* (pages 87-88) for picture-story book suggestions.

Chapter 6
Involving children in writing

Put it in writing

Opportunities for writing occur throughout the entire school day. Not only should teachers provide a time for children to write each day, but they should seize upon appropriate writing opportunities arising from every area of the curriculum.

"Put it in writing," is the catch-cry of one Year 3 class: "We write notes to our parents, letters to the Principal, to the canteen, the class next door. We write our thoughts after observations in Science or after listening to a piece of music. We write labels, captions, posters. There are hundreds of situations which come up in a day which lend themselves to all types of writing."

Each of these situations will have a different purpose for writing, involving different subjects and therefore different "registers". In Social Studies, for instance, situations will arise when there is a purpose for children to write reports, letters, diaries, biographies, tables, time-lines, captions, posters, etc.

Write with the class

Teachers often *read* to, and with, their children; thus there are regular demonstrations of reading behaviour for them to use as models. This is not always true of writing. We need to create opportunities which will allow children to observe teachers writing. One teacher who does this is Joan Hoyle at Ramsgate Public School (NSW): "I find that children are interested to see me putting ideas together in writing. It is good to let them see me struggling with sentences to get them right. Sometimes I ask children to help me with the composition of certain things, such as excursion notes, using the board. I often write a few lines of my own at the start of writing sessions. Once, when having trouble with a poem, I was surprised when one of the boys offered me a collection of Spike Milligan verses to use as models! The idea worked, and the children were delighted."

Publish for a variety of audiences

There are many ways of publishing children's writing, e.g. as posters, books, labels or letters. The reason for publishing is to make the writer's work available to potential readers. Publishing provides the motivation for children to correctly edit, rework, polish and finally proof-read their pieces so that they may communicate ideas clearly for others to read. Published work should be incor-

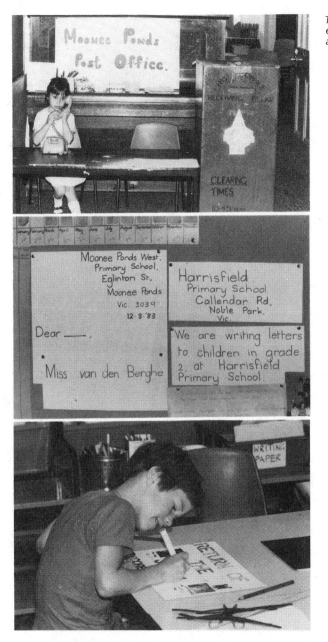

The children at Moonee Ponds West (Vic.) write enthusiastically, knowing their work has a real purpose and a definite audience.

porated into the general reading resources used in the classroom. One effect of this is that the children see that their efforts are associated with the work of professional writers and are valued in their own right. Thus do children come to perceive themselves as writers.

Publish for quality

At Moonee Ponds West (Victoria) the upper-primary children publish their polished pieces by neatly hand-writing the text and adding simple illustrations. These are placed in a class library for all to read. However, when a particularly good piece of writing is produced, the author is invited to publish it in a more sophisticated form. This may be as a "big book", a well-illustrated picture book, or in any other form. In order to determine how the work will be presented, the young author, in consultation with the teacher, makes decisions about the size and shape of the book, the type of illustrations appropriate for the text, the style of lettering to be used, and the layout. Many standard picture books are consulted as models, and much discussion ensues about such matters as whether to write in gold pen on black paper; whether to use collage or paint; whether to highlight particular words; indeed, whether to illustrate every page at all. The author chooses three or four helpers who will assist in making these decisions as well as doing some of the art work. The author continues to refine and polish the text. Sometimes, explicit detail in the illustrations will mean the text can be modified. Similarly, the art work may need modification in the light of changes in the text. The quality of the finished work is often very high indeed.

Marcia Saunders, a teacher at Moonee Ponds West, sees time spent on this publishing process as being well worth while: "The children gain insights into the way in which professional writers work, and they see the richness that illustrations can provide. A simple narrative about an outing to a French restaurant was enhanced by the humour in the illustrations. Time is provided for these projects during library and art and craft periods, as well as during language workshops. It takes some children a couple of weeks and others a whole term to produce finished books. The children really treasure them and insist that they be displayed in a prominent place in the classroom. I am continually amazed at the effort they put into these books, and the quality they produce."

Ingenuity produces some remarkable work at Reservoir East. Photography is used to include pupils themselves—along with Princess Diana—in this scene from an original fantasy (above). It also allows for the reproduction of things like clay engraving, in this book about the arrival of a new baby brother (below).

```
Mum told us his name was Lionel
and his second name was Barry
after my dad.
We stayed for about an hour,
then it was time to go.
```

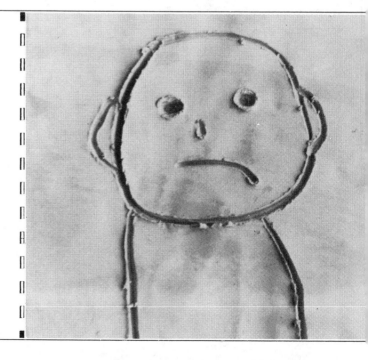

Publication provides purpose for writing.

Publish in a variety of forms

Rene Holmes of Wilkins Public School (NSW) encourages her Year 3 class to think of as many ways as they can to publish. On St Valentines Day they produced and sent cards to teachers on the staff. For the school camp they wrote and designed posters (in several languages) which were displayed around the school and local community to inform parents and seek sponsorship.

Robyn Legge's Year 2 class researched, tested and finally wrote-up their favourite recipes. They made multiple copies of these and sold them at their Bonnet Bay (NSW) school fete.

Jill Sweeting's Year 6 class, as part of a Social Studies unit on Leisure, produced an illustrated travel brochure to attract prospective customers to their imaginary holiday resort. Her children at Sylvania Heights Public School (NSW) had to provide a tourist map, descriptions of attractions, and directions on how to get to their resort, with details of costs and accommodation.

In all of the above writing situations, children had time to draft, revise, edit and proof-read their writing.

Marketing the product

The enterprising children at Reservoir East Primary School (Vic.) produce their own series of books called *Resa Kids*, which are widely used as reading material throughout the school. These little books are modelled on Lorraine Wilson's *City Kids* (Nelson) series and are published in multiple copies and sold to other schools in the area, or to any interested parties. While the proceeds are used to fund further publishing, the young authors, being accepted as such, thus know that their contributions are valued in their own right.

The children at Reservoir East publish and market their own Resa Kids books modelled on Lorraine Wilson's City Kids series.

For further reading

The Primary English Teaching Association has produced a number of books and *Primary English Notes* (PENs) on the subject of involving children in writing. Teachers will find the following publications to be an invaluable source of further ideas:

Turbill, Jan   *No Better Way to Teach Writing!* (P.E.T.A., 1982)
Now, We Want to Write! (P.E.T.A., 1983)

Walshe, R. D.   *Every Child Can Write!* (P.E.T.A., 1981)
Donald Graves in Australia; "Children want to write . . ." (P.E.T.A., 1981)

Chapter 7

Reading and writing: helping children to make the links

Shared book experience

INTRODUCTION

Shared book experience is a whole-class co-operative learning activity which is not unlike the bedtime story situation. It involves a daily time set aside for reading and re-reading favourite rhymes, songs, poems, chants and stories to and with children in order to demonstrate that reading is a pleasurable and meaningful experience.

A session with beginners might start with everyone reading a couple of familiar rhymes and singing a few songs, the words of which have been copied onto large sheets of cardboard or overhead transparencies visible to all. Thus, the children are simultaneously exposed to written as well as the oral forms of language. The teacher points to the words as they read, in order to demonstrate basic print concepts, as well as to ensure that children read in unison. Then the teacher re-reads one or two previously introduced stories, pausing to make occasional teaching points, and inviting the children to "read along", "clap along", use a

simple action, stomp in time or participate in some way. Then a new story is introduced. This story may be re-read a couple of times while the children join in with a catchy refrain or act out the story line. Suitable art, craft, drama, writing or reading experiences follow.

BEDTIME STORY SITUATION

Before we examine shared book experience in more detail, it is useful to look at the bedtime story situation because of what it can teach us about the way in which some children learn. In this situation many children learn to read, even though there has been no conscious effort made to "teach" them. When analysing this situation the following factors can be identified.

- The stories are shared in a warm, supportive environment.
- It is usually a one-to-one situation which happens regularly.
- The child often chooses the story to be read.
- The adult reads the story to the child.
- Adult and child together interact with the printed page.

- The child freely participates in the reading of the story in any way he or she wishes.
- The focus is purely on relaxed enjoyment and following the story line.
- There is no expectation that the child will exhibit any "reading-like" behaviour, although, if this *does* happen, the adult expresses delight and the child receives strong, positive, encouraging response.
- There are no obligatory follow-up tasks.
- Later on, the child often "pretend reads" the story to a teddy, a doll or to self.
- Favourites are read over and over again.

All of Brian Cambourne's seven conditions for learning (Chapter 2) are evident in the above situation. Because so many children who have a background rich in such experiences are able to read before they begin school, teachers should consider attempting to replicate this successful home-learning environment within the constraints of their own classrooms. Shared book experience is one attempt to do this in the spirit of a number of the above characteristics.

STEPS IN USING A STORY FOR SHARED BOOK EXPERIENCE

The following steps show how the teacher can use a story to teach a great deal about reading and writing, while having fun too.

Step 1. Teacher selects a suitable story

It is essential that the children are able to see the text and pictures clearly. For whole-class work, an enlarged form of the book is necessary. If this is not available, the activity should be done in a small enough group to allow children to see the words in the book. The story needs to have the following features:

- appeal for, and impact on, children;
- an absorbing story line that is predictable;
- pictures which both support and enhance the text;
- a supportive structure, e.g. one which contains elements of rhyme, rhythm and repetition, which make the language predictable.

Step 2. Introduce the story

Show the children the cover and discuss the illustration, the author and the title. Invite the children to predict what they think the story might be about. Read the story dramatically to the children, showing obvious delight in both the story line and the language. (Just as obvious should be the fact that this will only be convincing if the teacher has chosen a story he or she genuinely enjoys.) Sometimes the teacher may pause to invite children to predict outcomes.

After reading, the teacher allows time for spontaneous reaction and comments. If appropriate, brief questioning about parts the children enjoyed most, or about the cumulative story line, or reasons why certain events took place, etc. may follow in a relaxed and unpressured manner.

Next, the teacher may ask the children to retell the story in their own words, using the pictures to either assist them or confirm their predictions. Alternatively, the teacher may focus on a repetitive element such as a phrase, a chant, or a chorus, inviting the children to join in when the story is re-read. The teacher should point to the words in the text as he or she re-reads, in order to demonstrate the conventions of print. It is essential that the children feel free *not* to participate verbally if they prefer not to. The less confident children may wish merely to listen at this stage. If the children are particularly keen on the story, they may choose to dramatise it, perhaps using simple props.

The emphasis so far is on reading for meaning and enjoyment.

Before moving on to the next step it is necessary to introduce three or four more stories in the above way so that interest is maintained and the children will have several books to call upon.

Step 3. Read the story again

Once the children have a store of books with which they are familiar, the teacher may ask them to choose a favourite to be re-read. During this and subsequent re-readings the teacher is aiming at achieving the following.

1. *Increased participation.* At first this may involve a simple hand action, percussion accompaniment, moving to the rhythm of the words in the story, etc. Ultimately, the teacher is expecting the children to "read along".

2. *Teaching about the format of books* and the conventions of print, through demonstrations. Such conventions include:

- front cover, back cover
- title
- page
- page turning

Shared book experience—demonstrating the conventions of print.

- words
- spaces
- left to right, top to bottom
- read the words, not the picture
- picture supports the text
- one-to-one correspondence between written and spoken word
- punctuation and its functions
- letter-sound relationships

3. *Teaching reading-strategies.* The activities done with the book will demonstrate such strategies as:
- Reading to discover meaning
- Predicting and self-correcting, using the context of the story and common sense, along with knowledge of language, and letter/sound relationships
- Reading with expression.

4. *Developing a sight vocabulary.* Words which interest the children, e.g. *Bommy-knocker* (from *The Hungry Giant*) and *caterpillar* (from *The Very Hungry Caterpillar*) are quickly learned. Words which are repeated frequently, e.g. *a, the, and, is,* are recognised when used in context. It is not necessary to drill words using flash-cards, as these will be learnt over time in the context of the many stories presented to the children. The constant exposure to words in this way enables children to learn a sight vocabulary effortlessly.

5. *Learning "phonics".* Using shared book experience as an approach, children can begin reading books from the very first day at school. They do not need to know any "phonics" to begin. They do need to know the sound-symbol system of written language eventually, but they can learn this while learning to read and write. They will learn the twenty-six letters in the English alphabet and the fact that these letters represent different sounds in different words. (It is useful to refer to letters by

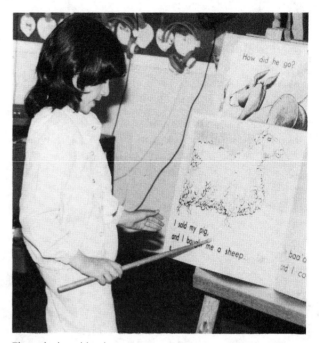

Through shared book experience children learn writing skills.

name because the name is consistent while the sound or sounds that many letters represent are not. Indeed many children already know letter names before they come to school.)

Through shared book reading, and their own writing, children explore and use the sound-symbol of language. They learn all the strategies they need for spelling in writing, and word attack in reading.

Step 4. Independent reading
The books introduced and read to the children in Step 2 should now all be available for the children to choose to read for themselves, the interest generated in the group situation usually being a

motivating force. In the case of "big books", normal-sized copies should be made available. For standard picture-story books introduced in a small group situation, it is necessary for children to have access to individual copies. (Many are available as inexpensive paperbacks, allowing for multiple copies to be purchased.)

One of the best ways to organise these books is in "book boxes". Empty ice-cream containers or cut-down wine casks make good boxes. There can be a box for each child or group of children. Everything included in the box should have been introduced and read previously to the children, and be at the children's independent reading level. The collection should be changed constantly. However, books removed from boxes should then be placed in the class library to enable children to return to old favourites whenever they want to.

There are many useful activities which can follow shared book experience. These should be done in small groups or individually. They include:
- "cloze" activities
- innovation on text
- creating "big books"
- writing
- string sentences.

For further reading on shared book experience see Don Holdaway's *The Foundations of Literacy* (Ashton Scholastic, 1979) and Andrea Butler's *The Story Box in the Classroom* (Rigby Education, 1984).

Innovating on text

"I find innovating on text an excellent way of teaching children about how sentences and stories work. They learn grammar, punctuation and spelling easily from this activity. It also helps them to write far more interesting stories of their own." — *David Malmgren*

Innovating on text involves making up a new sentence or story based on the structure of existing text. It is done by substituting words or phrases, adding words or phrases or even deleting them. Once one or two words are substituted, many other words in the text may need to be changed if the story, rhyme or poem is to continue to make sense. For instance, once the children in Lyn Walker's kindergarten class at Jannali (NSW) had changed the word *baa* to *moo* in "Baa, Baa, Black Sheep" they found it necessary to re-examine (i.e. re-read) the rhyme to decide what other words needed to be changed to ensure that the new version had consistency:

Moo, moo, white cow,
Have you any milk?
Moo, moo, moo, moo,
Three buckets full.
One for the boy,
One for the girl,
And one for the monster
Who lives down the drain.
Ahhhhhhh!

Innovating on sentences

Sue Harris
Illawong Public School (NSW)

I use sentences from children's writing, as well as from printed books, for activities designed to help children understand how language works, e.g. expanding and contracting sentences. After reading Jenny Wagner's book, *John Brown, Rose and the Midnight Cat* (Kestrel/Puffin) to my Year 5 children, we talked about the story line, why we liked it, and so on. Then we chose a sentence from the book to innovate on. I wrote on the board: "In the summer he sat under the pear tree with her".

I now asked the children to think of a phrase we could use to replace *in summer*. They suggested not only other seasons but alternatives such as *in Australia* or *at night*. I listed their suggestions underneath and asked the children to read the resulting new sentences. We talked about which ones were more meaningful, and why. We repeated this process for all of the other words or phrases in the sentence.

In summer	he	sat	under	the pear tree	with her.
In winter	John	lay	near	the oak tree	by Rose.
In autumn	the dog	walked	up	the hill	beside her.
In spring	the cat	played	behind	the house	with John.

On another occasion, after reading a story by a pupil of mine named Samir, I wrote one of his sentences on the board and we experimented with it. Our aim was to add other words or phrases which would make the sentence more informative. The sentence was: "The car stopped". Firstly, I asked the children to think of a word that might fit between *the* and *car*. They suggested *red, old, new, beautiful, shiny*. We repeated the process of fleshing out and changing, by substituting and expanding, other parts of the original skeletal sentence and ended up with the following sentences:

Because the light changed	the red car	stopped	in a hurry.
On Saturday	an old truck	started	suddenly.
When I braked	our new bus	swerved	off the road.
All of a sudden	John's BMX bike	skidded	into the mud.

After reading all the sentences and all the combinations of the word-clusters we could make, we talked about which ones were meaningful, and which ones would fit into Samir's story. He liked: "When I braked, the red car skidded into the mud".

We also tried putting two sentences together rather than expanding a single one. I wrote the following two sentences from Trang's story onto strips of paper: "I have a dog. He is big."

Firstly we read the whole story and then read the two sentences that I had copied out. Then I cut up the sentences, word by word, and asked the children to suggest ways in which I could put the words into a meaningful order. They quickly came up with: "I have a big dog". After doing these as a whole-class activity, I now can encourage the children to use the strategy with their own writing. They try it out on each other as they edit their work.

Innovating on stories

David Malmgren
Moonee Ponds West Primary School (Vic.)

I often have my Year 1 children innovating on whole stories as well as sentences. For instance, after hearing *The Big Toe* (Story Box) in a shared book session, some children suggested that we make up our own story on similar lines. Accordingly, while others moved off to various reading and writing tasks, a group of eight children decided to work with me on this task.

First, we re-read the story, discussing the pictures and the words and the way in which they had been arranged. The children noticed that for the refrain "Who's got my big toe?" the print gradually enlarges in size. We discussed reasons why the writer might have done this, and then re-read the story aloud, using "small" voices to match the small print, but increasing the volume as the print increased in size. Then we acted it out. After further discussion I covered the word *toe* with a card and asked what other part of the body could be substituted. Away we went, as writers, on *our* story, "The Big Ear".

I wrote the new story in front of the children, using large sheets of paper. Substituting was simple. The basic pattern was very easy and few words needed to be changed to retain meaning. The children decided to change the places where the voice was heard: *by the gate* became *by the*

A read-together book.

Then something away down the road said, "Who's got my big toe?"

4

brick wall; in the hall became in the kitchen; on the stairs became by the indoor plants. Finally, it was decided that the *old woman* should become *the old man*. This meant going back through our large draft and changing it where necessary.

I hung the story draft on the wall for children to read. Later, we made a "big book" (illustrated by the authors, of course) and the children had great delight in reading the story to the whole class and to others in the school. Rooms echoed with choruses of, "Who's got my big ear?"

The Big Ear
An old man found a big ear
and he took it home.
Then something away down the road said,
"Who's got my big ear?"
Then something by the brick wall said,
"Who's got my big ear?" _ _ _

The "big book" proved to be a popular addition to our large collection of "home-made" books, all of which are eagerly sought-after for overnight borrowing and free reading. Not all the innovations we do are published as "big books". Many stay only in draft form. *(David describes more about creating "Big Books" on p. 72)*

Sentence strips and word banks

Deborah Jones
Moonee Ponds West Primary School (Vic.)

As an aid to the teaching of reading to my 5 year-olds, I use "sentence strips". I begin by asking the children to choose one of the stories they have written, or drawn, during writing time. I write their story (or sentence—their stories at this stage usually consist of only one sentence) on a long strip of pre-cut cardboard, 10 cm × 80 cm. Nicole's picture and story is: *"We had to take my cat Moggie to the vet".*

We discuss this story and the child reads it several times. We then discuss various points of interest, such as where the story begins and ends, what is a word, the full stop and its function, and the spaces between words. Then I write the sentence onto another strip, being sure it matches the first strip exactly. We cut the second strip into "word cards". This now becomes a valuable word-matching activity which is based on the children's own language. Children add to these sentences whenever they want something written out for them (i.e. published). Some may do as many as three a week. Each day, children play with their strips and words, matching the words to the master-strip and then reading to a friend or to me. Strips are easily stored by using a coat-hanger, plastic bag for the word cards, and a peg for attaching the strips, and plastic bag, to the coat-hanger.

After children have about four or five of these strips, they choose one that they can read and I write it into a book. The children then illustrate these and thus develop a collection of stories which they can read to any interested person. The activity soon becomes a smooth cycle of making up new sentences and adding old ones into the story book. I use a great deal of cardboard strips but, as we do so much with them, it is worthwhile.

As children are working so closely with language which is meaningful to them, they soon begin to recognise some of the words, especially those which interest them, such as *Moggie*, and others which are repeated often, such as *the* or *to*. Once they recognise a word, I write it onto smaller cards, which they keep as individual "word banks". We store these in cut-down empty milk cartons (soaked in bleach for a few days to remove the smell) which I cover with Contact adhesive film and label with their names. It is surprising how quickly this bank of known words grows.

LEFT: Rachel has her own "word bank".

BELOW LEFT: The teacher prepares a duplicate sentence strip to be cut into separate word cards.

BELOW: Making a sentence strip from word-cards.

Once the concept of a word has been developed, the children can begin to work with their "word bank" by classifying and categorising words in a variety of ways or by making up new sentences, which they read to each other. They bring their "word banks" to group activities, and I may, for instance, ask them to find all the words they own which start with *w* or end with *ing* or *t*, etc. They like pulling out their words and reading them to the other children. The children are learning "sight words", "phonics" and spelling through enjoyable, meaningful activities. They love it and often choose to play with them whenever they have free time. Sometimes our day is just not long enough.

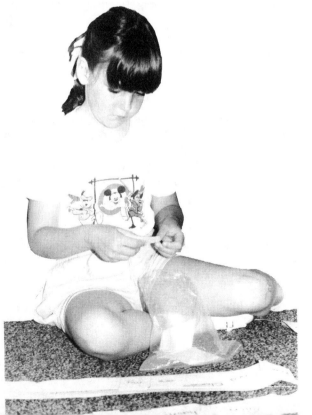

Creating class "big books"

Many teachers report that, along with shared book experience, the creating of class "big books" plays a major role in developing the children's reading, writing and oral-language skills. These books are simply large-sized books containing texts written on large sheets of paper or cardboard, in a print size which is large enough for children to see, illustrated and put together as a "big book". Often, the pages are displayed along the wall at child height so that they may be easily read. Every week at least one book is created in this way by different groups in classrooms at Moonee Ponds West.

The stimulus for a "big book" arises from two major sources:

1. Existing literature. Familiar stories, poems, rhymes, chants and songs (including those introduced through shared book experience) can be used as the text for the book, the children adding their own illustrations. The same sources provide models on which the children can innovate to create different versions.

2. A real or vicarious experience. This experience should have been shared by a small group, if not the whole class. It may have been planned, be connected with the class theme, or it may have been spontaneous. It may have occurred before, during, or after school hours, e.g.

- *A Wet Day at School*
- *Making Pancakes*
- *Growing Herbs in our Room*
- *The Grand Final*
- *Pets*

Creating "big books" using existing stories

Leanna Traill
Te Papapa School (Auckland, NZ)

When we decide to create a "big book" from a story my infants class likes, I write the text onto large strips of paper or cardboard, in front of the children. I encourage them to continually refer to the original book to check that I haven't made any mistakes. We read and re-read the text, discussing sequence, characters, spelling and punctuation. Each child is asked to illustrate one of the pages from the book. Once the drawings or paintings are finished, the children bring their work and sit together on the floor. I then present them with the strips, and together they match their pictures and the text before arranging the story into the correct sequence. I encourage them to assist each other, using the original book as their sole reference. As a result, the children are soon able to match the text to their pictures, and to arrange their stories into correct sequence, without needing to consult me.

The children's pictures, and appropriate text, are pasted onto large sheets of cardboard and displayed at child height along the wall. The children are encouraged to read this wall story any time they wish. They love to use my pointer and play "teacher" with their friends. After about one week the story is taken down and a title page and cover prepared by the children. These books are great favourites, even though the children did not originate them, because they feel a sense of ownership.

Lynne Smith
Sans Souci Public School (NSW)

Creating "big books" using existing stories is a useful activity for infants classes, but it is equally useful for older readers, as I found with my new Year 3-4 composite class. They disliked reading lessons, and I was beginning to dislike them too. The children had had several years of learning to read through old-style flash-card drill and phonic activities. They perceived reading as boring and meaningless, and their attempts to read demonstrated this. They liked it whenever I read to them, but when I asked them to read they began showing signs of "avoidance behaviour". I was desperate for some educational reading activity which would not only hold their interest and help them with their writing but which could demonstrate that reading could be fun. Making our own "big books" was the answer to the problem.

I knew that the children in the infants classes at our school were in need of more "big books", so I suggested to my class that we make them one, using *Mrs Wishy-Washy*, one of the books in the "Story Box" collection. I began by reading the story to my class and found that they liked it as much as I knew the young ones did.

I borrowed enough copies of *Mrs Wishy-Washy* to enable my class to share one copy between two children. I gave these out and we read the story through several times. So far, so good. I then copied the text from each page onto strips as they watched. (I made sure I didn't number the strips and I deliberately left out certain punctuation so that they could remind me to put it in.)

When all the strips were ready, we discussed what illustrations needed to go with each strip. In this way, the children had to think about the meaning and sequence of the story; this required a number of re-readings of the text. The children were reading without realising it. My insistence that we put the strips and small books aside for the day was met with some protest!

The next day the children nagged me to get started again on our "big book". Out came the mixed-up strips and the small books. We read through the strips again and arranged them in correct sequence. The children didn't need to use the small book as a reference but we read it anyway. We checked the spelling and punctuation on the strips. Then, working in pairs, the children took strips and a large sheet of paper and went to their tables to paint the appropriate picture. Discussions between them centred around the sequence, the message of the story and the audience they were making the book for. A few decided that their pictures would not do, and so they started again. I reminded them that writers and illustrators often needed to do a second draft and that it was perfectly acceptable for this to happen.

When their paintings were dry, we had to once again read the strips and match the text to the appropriate picture. We pasted the strips onto the paintings and I stapled the "big book" together. The children couldn't wait to show the kindergarten class so, before we attached the cover and title page, two children were elected to go and read the story to the younger ones. As the week went by, all my children had a turn at reading to the kindergarten class. (They kept bringing *our* "big book" back, however, arguing that "those little kids might tear it"!)

During the following term we made many such books, both big and little, supposedly for the younger children to read. My class now began to write and produce books on all sorts of other topics for the younger children. These books were often modelled on the "big books" we had made as a class. Although they were for the younger children, my class never actually gave these books away. They spent a good deal of time reading them themselves.

Through this activity, my children were confidently learning the language skills they needed without realising it—and I wasn't about to tell them.

Creating "big books" by innovating on existing stories

Bronwen Scarffe
Deer Park North Primary School (Vic.)

Sometimes after my Grade 1 children have particularly enjoyed a shared book experience of a story, or a rhyme, chant or song, they choose to innovate on it to make our own class "big books". Once we have made these as class or group activities, the children often use them as models for their own writing. In fact, if the children are having trouble finding something to write about, I encourage them to do this. The "big books" created in class become most useful resources for reading, spelling and writing.

Creating "big books" using real or vicarious experiences

David Malmgren
Moonee Ponds West Primary School (Vic.)

Once the topic is chosen, I help the children develop a story by discussing, questioning, and suggesting, with reference to characters, plot-sequence, vocabulary, etc. The writing task is simplified because I do the actual handwriting, while the composing is shared by the group. A recent story, composed by the whole class over a period of two weeks, was entitled "Excuses, Excuses, Excuses", prompted by the number of late arrivals each morning. After getting the opening sentence down, we added to it as we needed to:

People in Grade 1, Room 2, are ALWAYS LATE!
Any individuals who arrived after the 9 a.m. bell were required to explain the cause of their lateness. The group formulated a sentence about each, and thus a cumulative list of late-comers and their excuses was built up, e.g.

Daniel arrived at 9.30. "Sorry I'm late D.M., but I couldn't find my other desert boot."
Corey was late. "Sorry D.M., but Mum wouldn't get out of the bath."
Kate was late because her sister wouldn't write her lunch order out.
Belinda was late. "My brother got his bag and hit me on the head," she said.

The problem of how to end the story, when it was obvious that it was becoming too long, was solved by a child who made the (very popular) suggestion that the whole class might be *early*, while I would be late! The next day, when I walked into our classroom just before 9 a.m., I was surprised by twenty-eight smiling faces, all waiting for me to arrive. They chorused with cheeky grins: "What's YOUR excuse?" I was speechless—and now we had our perfect ending:

D.M. was late.
The children said: "What's YOUR excuse?"

D.M. was so surprised
He fainted!

I placed our story-draft on the wall, where it hung for a week before we re-wrote it, illustrated it, made a cover and title-page for it and finally sewed it together.

Why make "big books"?

Many reading, writing and oral skills can be learned by children while engaged in planning and making "big books". Through this activity, teachers can assist children to learn such things as the following:

* the nature of print, and its arrangement from left to right and top to bottom;
* the need to leave spaces between words;
* the convention of using a capital letter at the beginning of a sentence;
* the need to select the most appropriate words for particular points in the story;
* the various aspects of punctuation, e.g. full stops, question marks, commas, quotation marks;
* spelling, through asking such questions as:
  — *What letter do you think the word _____ will begin with?*
  — *What sound do you hear next in this word? What letter(s) do you think make that sound?*
  — *Does this word look right?*
  — *How else could I write _____?*
* the concept of writing as a process rather than a product. By drafting stories in front of them, the teacher allows the children to see how a writer revises by adding or subtracting information, altering individual words and general arrangement. Through asking questions such as, "Are you happy with the way our story starts? Is this part necessary? Does it have anything to do with the title?", children learn the importance of careful construction.

Published "big books" have many additional uses:
* "Cloze" activities, oral or written, using initial letter clues, final letter clues, or with whole words deleted.
* Small books can be made from them, in multiple copies if necessary, illustrated by children.
* Shared book experience.
* Sentence strips for sequencing, for re-arranging, for copying, etc.
* Word study
  (a) The story may be scanned to discover words with similarities, e.g. those which start with *ch*, end with *ing*, or contain *and* within them. These words can be listed on charts for further reference, or put on cards for games.
  (b) Individual words from a story can be written on cards and the whole class or groups of children can be asked to sort them according to letters, sounds, meaning.

Getting "inside the author's head"

Marilyn Woolley and Keith Pigdon
Melbourne College of Advanced Education

In order for children to write well, it is important for them to learn to "read as a writer". The activity outlined below is designed to help older children try to "get inside the author's head" in order to understand

- the author's possible intentions in writing the piece,
- the message the author might be trying to convey,
- the background information he or she needed,
- choice of register.

In classrooms where this activity has been done frequently, it is apparent that children have made links between good literature models and their own writing.

There are many excellent books in the field of literature which can involve children as readers and which offer good opportunities for them to speculate on the processes the authors might have gone through in order to create the finished work. We will focus on two Australian books, Colin Thiele's short novel, *Magpie Island* (Rigby) and Ted Greenwood's picture-story book, *Everlasting Circle* (Hutchinson), both of which we have used with upper primary classes.

Magpie Island, by Colin Thiele

1. Reading/listening in order to be involved in a good story

The children read the book silently over a given time period, or listen to it being read by the teacher as a daily serial. Upon completion, the story is discussed, individual responses and opinions being encouraged. The idea is to ascertain the level of comprehension reached in the intitial reading. If

COLIN THIELE / ROGER HALDANE

MAGPIE ISLAND

the children seem to have grasped the essential points of the story, they are now ready to analyse it.

2. Preparation

The teacher copies out a couple of passages (chosen by either the teacher or the children) from the book onto large sheets of paper or overhead transparencies so that all the children can see them. These passages should be about a main character, the setting, a main issue or the introductory paragraph of a chapter. We chose the following:

> The shoreline of the island came nearer still. Magpie was done now, staggering about in the air, tumbling pitifully. But he didn't give in. And at last, blinded by spray and numb with exhaustion, he reached the shore and flopped down. He was so worn out that he couldn't even keep his feet as he touched the sand. A wind-gust caught him and sent him rolling over and over up the beach of the little cove like an old feather duster until he was stopped by a big stone above the tide mark. For

a minute he lay there stunned. Then he picked himself up and struggled round into a little hollow on the other side. There he lay for hours like a dead bird while the daylight drained away and the darkness came up out of the sea and rolled over the little island.

But strange things began to happen with the coming of the night. The dusk had hardly fallen when the water started to churn and stir. An army of little grey ghosts popped up out of the sea and, standing upright, hurried up the beach. They waddled as they went, as if taking part in a fast walking race.

The teacher prepares questions which will help the children "get inside the author's head" for that particular part of the book. Aspects covered include semantic cue system (content), syntactic cue system (language used) and grapho-phonic system (punctuation, spelling). These questions may be for teacher's use only, and later may be copied out for children to use during small group discussion.

3. Reading as a writer

The following day a small group of between eight to ten children have a more in-depth discussion in order to try to "get inside Colin Thiele's head". We begin by imagining that we *are* the author, in an attempt to discover the kind of writing process the author might have gone through. First, we re-read the passages aloud and talk about them in relation to the whole book. Then the children are asked to answer the prepared questions, using only the selected extracts for reference.

The following table shows, in the middle column, the questions we asked the children. It also indicates, on the left, the particular aspect of the reading-writing process being covered. The column on the right explains why that particular question is useful in terms of learning "to read like a writer".

WHAT (Item)	HOW (Teaching Strategies)	WHY (Purpose)
1. CONTENT—ideas, knowledge of the world (*semantic cue* system of information).	1. What did he need to know about magpies? List items: their song, nesting habits, territories, predators, flying habits, wing span.	1. Imagine and discuss the kind of behaviour writers engage in.
	2. What did he need to know about Eyre Peninsula of South Australia, and the local seabirds? List items: the peninsula and its distinctive features, the location of the island, the birds' behaviour (high pitched shrieks, penguins arriving at dusk), Australian animals (the bandicoot), local fishing.	2. Demonstrate that writers *control* their information.
		3. Discuss range of possible resources.
	3. How would he get to know these things? • Personal experience and knowledge: *I grew up in country areas where the white-backed magpie was my companion every day* (Foreword). • Many hours of research: reading, observing, studying maps, asking people.	4. Model questions that children can ask themselves when drafting and revising.
		5. Demonstrate that writing takes time.
	4. What do you think are Colin Thiele's feelings, opinions and values? (N.B. Magpie has no name.) The relationship between some people and birds, e.g. "sportsmen" used magpies for target practice.	6. Demonstrate that many problems need to be solved.
		7. Allow children to realise that they are emulating adults.

WHAT (Item)	HOW (Teaching Strategies)	WHY (Purpose)
2. LANGUAGE — knowledge of how language works: structure, cohesion, order (*syntactic cue* system of information).	1. How did he choose to write the book? (Register) • It's a story full of action. Appropriate language is chosen to suit his particular purpose. • Sequence of events follow on from each other. • We can make reasonable predictions as we read/listen to the story. 2. How did he choose to present the information? • Use of pictorial information in form of paintings and drawings by Roger Haldane. Key sentence or phrase repeated. • Setting out. • Choice of title.	1. Stress author's likely meanings and intentions in his use of language. 2. Skills taught in a meaningful context. 3. Provide models of how language works, how it is used and how it looks. 4. Demonstrate the use of the page.
Specific analysis of particular passages.	3. His use of language to depict concepts of time, e.g., . . . *while the daylight drained away and the darkness came up out of the sea* . . . 4. His range of sentence beginnings. 5. His particular devices, e.g. — *like an old feather duster* — *an army of little grey ghosts.* 6. His use of strong words to evoke meaning, e.g. *staggering, struggling, tumbling pitifully.*	5. Discuss skills in a meaningful context. 6. Extend knowledge of words through demonstrating their use in a given context. 7. Provide models of syntax for children's future use.

3. SURFACE FEATURES — knowledge of conventions, punctuations, spelling strategies (*graphophonic* cue system of information).	1. His use of "conventions", e.g. apostrophes for abbreviations (*couldn't, didn't, what's*).
	2. Studying specific words he has used:
	• visual patterns within words, e.g. double letters (sta**gg**ering, sto**pp**ed, ho**ll**ow); clusters (is**land**, n**ear**er).
	• morphemic — exhaust**ion**
	— shoreline, windgust
	— hard**ly**, pitifu**lly**
	• Sound patterns, e.g.
	— pronunciation of "ea"; f**ea**ther, r**ea**ched
	— representation of common sound with different letters, e.g.
	(i) exh**au**stion (ii) **e**ven
	    for army
	    shore pitifully
		1. Model the conventions children need to learn.
		2. Demonstrate organizational strategies for children's future use. Allow them to become self regulatory in their use of checking devices when proof-reading.
		3. Extend children's knowledge of how words work.
		4. Demonstrate that letters only have a pronunciation in the context of the given word.
		5. Demonstrate that the sounds of our language can be represented by a variety of letters and letter combinations.

TED GREENWOOD

Everlasting Circle, by Ted Greenwood

Comparison and contrasts can be drawn with this book, which deals with similar ideas and information. This is a shorter book, a story of a shearwater (mutton bird) chick, and it could be read in one session to highlight the balance of the words and the pictorial information. In using this book in any teaching situation it would be inappropriate to separate the text from the pictures.

We have done so only for demonstration purposes here:

No enemy found this egg.
Safely
In the dark of a burrow it lay
warmed
through fifty-three days
fifty-four nights
before its shell cracked
and a chick emerged,
all in the dark of a burrow.

Too late
a visitor came searching for prey
too late
to devour this chick
growing so fat and downy;
feed after feed
feed after feed after feed
and then
no more
no more easy feeds
or parental warmth
alone now
to find life beyond
the mouth of the burrow
where others
called.

. . .

The long flight again—
each year the great journey north
each year the great journey home,
unerringly
back to her island
to her own burrow,
another egg
another chick
and again another journey
yet again
and again and again
the rhythm of the flock
for the rest of her time.

To begin the general discussion, we would use the same predictable focus question: What did Ted Greenwood need to know before he could write *Everlasting Circle?*

WHAT (Item)	HOW (Teaching Strategies)	WHY (Purpose)
1. CONTENT	1. What did he need to know about shearwater chicks? 2. Highlight the focus on the female, her life cycle, incubation, her nesting habits (burrow), migration patterns, predators, her role as a parent. 3. Discuss Ted Greenwood's decision not to name the island. What do you think were his intentions in doing so? 4. Discuss, also, the symbolism of the everlasting circle. What do you think this might mean. (The author uses the same symbolism in his book *V. I. P., Very Important Plant*.) 5. How would he get to know these things? • Personal experience and knowledge. Discuss the amount of time Ted Greenwood must have spent observing and sketching the shearwaters in order to gain this knowledge. • These observations backed up by research (reading, asking people). 6. What do you think are Ted Greenwood's thoughts and feelings? Discuss how his gentle, sensitive story demonstrates that he feels very strongly about birds and, in particular, shearwaters. He highlights their battles with the elements and predators. Discuss his emphasis on the rhythm of life, the everlasting circle.	1. Imagine and discuss the kind of behaviour writers engage in. 2. Allow children to contrast information used with that in *Magpie Island*. 3. Focus on this author's specific intentions to stress *control* of information. 4. Discuss range of possible resources. 5. Model questions that children can ask of themselves when drafting and revising. 6. Demonstrate similarities of writing behaviour of the two authors. 7. Demonstrate that writing takes a great deal of time.
2. LANGUAGE — knowledge of how language works: structure, cohesion, order (syntactic cue system of information).	1. How did Ted Greenwood choose to write this book? (Register) • It is a story, in which the message is made clear through the use of poetic expression. • Sequence of events flows. 2. How did he choose to present the information? • Sensitivity portrayed through use of poetic form and delicate drawing. • The pictures and the language are in harmony with each other. We have to pause over both of them. • Pictures also give additional information, e.g. about the visitor "searching for prey".	1. Stress author's likely meaning and intent in his use of language. 2. Skills are taught in a meaningful context. 3. Provide model of how language works, how it is used and how it looks.

WHAT (Item)	HOW (Teaching Strategies)	WHY (Purpose)

Specific analysis of particular passages.	3. His use of language to depict concepts of time, e.g.
	— *warmed through fifty-three days*
	— *each year the great journey north*
	
	4. Range of sentence beginnings.
	
	5. Particular devices, e.g. **repetition** to evoke images of everlasting circles:
	— *feed after feed*
	  feed after feed after feed
	— *another egg*
	  another chick
	  and again another journey.
	
	6. *Strong words to evoke author's meaning, e.g.*
	  devour
	  unerringly
		4. Draw contrasts with *Magpie Island* to demonstrate how information can be presented in a variety of ways.
		
		5. Discuss skills in a meaningful context.
		
		6. Provide models of syntax for children's future use.
		
		7. Extend knowledge of words through demonstrating their use in a given context.

3. SURFACE FEATURES—
—knowledge of conventions, spelling (grapho-phonic cue system of information).
	1. His use of "conventions", e.g. punctuation.
	
	2. Studying specific words, e.g.
	• Visual patterns
	— of text itself
	— within words:
	  bu**rrow**
	  pa**rent**al
	  de**vour**
	• Morphemic analysis, e.g.
	  stretch**ed**
	  safe**ly**
	  unerring**ly**
	• Sound patterns, e.g.
	— pronunciation of "ou" in:
	  f**ou**nd
	  thr**ou**gh
	  f**ou**r
	  m**ou**th
	  j**ou**rney
	— representation of common sound with different letters, e.g.
	  safe**ly** **la**y
	  prey a**gai**n
		1. Model the conventions children need to learn.
		
		2. Demonstrate organizational strategies for children's future use. Allow them to become self-regulatory in their use of checking devices when proof-reading.
		
		3. Extend children's knowledge of how words work.
		
		4. Demonstrate that letters only have a pronunciation in the context of a given word.
		
		5. Demonstrate that the sounds of our language can be represented by a variety of letters and letter combinations.

Helping children make links with their own writing

Jo Parry
Reservoir East Primary School (Vic.)

With my composite Grade 4/5/6, I try to help the children to make the links between reading activities and their own writing, in front of the children. Whilst demonstrating the writing process I ask myself, aloud, the same sorts of questions which children ask in analysing the work of other writers when attempting to get "inside the author's head".

During this activity I find that there are opportunities to demonstrate, in a meaningful context, all of the following:

Use of appropriate information

* Successful authors usually write about things which they know about or are interested in.
* Writers sometimes outline, for themselves, the things they *do* know about the topic they intend to write about. This helps them realise what they don't know and tells them what they need to find out.
* Writers may consult various sources to gain information.
* Writers need to select characters appropriate to the setting and the plot.
* Events need to be ordered in a logical sequence.
* Writers add or delete information in order to make their meaning clear.

Editing and publishing strategies

* paragraphing
* inserting new information
* crossing out
* cutting and pasting
* using arrows
* asterisks
* using the margin
* layout
* publishing formats
* use of illustrations

Knowledge of the writing process

* rehearsing
* recalling experience
* selecting information
* imagining an experience
* putting feelings into writing
* deciding upon the main idea or ideas
* spelling
* editing
* revising
* reorganising
* using effective opening sentences
* concluding a piece decisively and satisfyingly
* consulting others
* being aware of audience

The children in my classroom are able to demonstrate an awareness of these aspects of the writing process. Here is what 11-year-old Cassie has to say:

I like the way we learn from others. We treat everyone as an author in our room. Children are authors, Miss Parry is an author, other kids are authors, and other people are authors. So what we do is we study how all these authors write. Sometimes we put up a person's draft on a piece of paper. Sometimes Miss Parry writes a draft. We all help to make it better. Sometimes after shared-book, a couple of us or Miss Parry, have to write up part of that book on a piece of paper. We look at lead sentences, strong words and punctuation. We have to ask ourselves: "What did Colin Thiele need to know and think about before he could publish that book?" We have to imagine we are him and go backwards.

Sometimes we actually ask an author to come for an interview. Ted Greenwood came and Michael Dugan and Lorraine Wilson. We could talk to them author to author. It's good, I remember lots of things they said because I did the same thing in my drafts. I think we're lucky because we can get help from other people. They think writing's pretty hard and perhaps its because they've got to do it by themselves and think up all the questions to ask themselves.

Children can use printed books as models for their own writing.

Using literature to help children edit their own writing

Once children perceive themselves as writers, through daily writing opportunities, and have gained insight into how other writers write, through their daily reading opportunities, teachers can use literature to help children improve their own writing.

Many young children write stories or reports which contain far too much irrelevant or superfluous information—they are intent on telling more than the reader wants to know. Buried in what is written may be one or two events or statements which are central to what the young writer wants to share with an audience. How can we help the child focus on a single main idea? Take, for example, the following piece, "On Sunday", written by 8-year-old Sharon, of Wilkins Public School (NSW):

> On Sunday.
> on Sunday we went for a pinck and we had to Wat for our luch then we went in the rivea ther was a Tarzanrop and my friend called Tracey she went in the worter and my ather friend called shan he father put him in the worter then all off them had to go home we went home in the dark and we got home we had dina it was tuckyfid chicken for dina.

When Sharon's teacher, Jane Mowbray, asked her what had been the most exciting thing to happen on her picnic, Sharon answered: "Swinging on the Tarzan rope". Jane pointed out that Sharon had hardly mentioned the rope in her writing. As a result, Sharon described the incident in some detail, causing Jane to conclude: "You had a really exciting time at the river with that rope, didn't you? Why don't you just write about that part? But before you start, let's look at how other writers do it."

Jane took a "City Kids" book and showed Sharon and a few other children, who were having a similar problem, how the author, Lorraine Wilson, had set out her story. There were one or two sentences per page, along with illustrations. They discussed the sequence and looked at how the author had started straight into the story, and gone straight on, finishing at the end of the incident. They then took Sharon's story again and discussed where it could start and end to better effect. Sharon decided that it should begin at the point where they started playing while waiting for the barbecue to cook, the appropriate ending being at the point when the food was actually cooked. The modified story would mainly be about what did happen with the Tarzan rope.

Jane then suggested that Sharon might like to draw the pictures first, so she ruled up a few pages, each into four sections. Sharon drew her pictures on the right, leaving the left-hand section for the text. After all the drawings were complete, she wrote the appropriate captions, with a directness which was lacking in her first draft (although that first draft had been a necessary start).

Starting and ending stories

Pam McIntyre-Smith
Wilkins Public School (NSW)

Children often find it difficult to find ways into their own stories or to vary the ways in which they commence them. Literature provides many different models, and it is useful to have children consider the way in which professional authors struc-

ture their opening paragraphs. I sometimes list, on the board, the types of story openings (or "leads") commonly used by my Year 5 children. When they compare these with examples taken from library books they soon notice the range and variety of possible alternatives. This is enlightening for those children who monotonously lead in with, for example, adverbial phrases and clauses of time (e.g. *During the holidays . . .; One day in July . . .; When I went to Grandma's house . . .*).

I ask the children to consider which openings from books they could use in their own work. I get them to start again, trying some out. I usually ask them to do this part in pairs so they can assist each other to decide which lead is best. The aim of the activity is to make the children more aware of models which they could use in their current or future writing. We usually hang on the wall a chart containing opening sentences from books so that the children can refer to it for future stories. We add to this chart as the year goes by. It becomes a constant reference for the children.

One of the greatest difficulties children have with their writing is in knowing how and when to end. All teachers are familiar with the unimaginative *and then I went to bed* or *and then I woke up* endings. To show how adult authors use endings effectively to clinch, round off or climax their stories, one Year 5 teacher likes to read picture-story book texts to her class, because many of these books end with surprising "punch-lines" which amuse and delight. An excellent example is Pamela Allen's *Who Sank the Boat?* (Nelson) which answers, only at the end, the question it keeps asking throughout the text.

Mem Fox's *Possum Magic* (Omnibus) is a story about the adventures of two possums. Mem ends her story by reiterating the conditions that Grandma Poss found were necessary for Hush to remain visible forever. My class discovered that it was necessary to look at the last paragraph (not just the last few words) and to relate that paragraph to the whole story-line in order to grasp its significance. By drawing the children's attention to the many ways which professional authors choose to end a story, they are made more aware of the importance of endings, and the way in which they are led up to, logically, by the text as a whole. In time, this will carry-over into their own writing.

Being a critical reader of one's own writing

Sue Doran
Wilkins Public School (NSW)

Sometimes it is difficult for children to understand why their finished writing does not seem clear to other readers. Writers can be too close to their own work to see it objectively. Teachers may need to help children stand back from their own writing in an effort to see it more critically. There are many reasons why children may find it difficult to edit their writing. Sometimes, if poor handwriting seems to be a barrier, I will type out the child's work, correcting all the spelling and punctuation, and sometimes type each new sentence on a new line. I always leave double spacing between the lines. Sometimes I type it out in sections which seem to go together. This is useful if the piece, as written, does not follow a logical sequence.

Presented with the typewritten version, young writers now become readers and it is surprising how quickly they pick up any confusions inherent in the original passage. For instance, ten-year-old Huy couldn't see why the message was unclear in his piece. He had first written it in Vietnamese, but was having difficulty with the translation into English. Huy's limited English was preventing him from

Courage
The story of Jakie Robisoin

Once upon a time,
there live a boys called Jackie Robinson he were black and his famerly were poor then one days he went home then they say we got a suprise for you said his mum so his mum gave him a basball ball tf Jackie like it very much but I it make out of wool so it different then the other basball ball. Jackie play with it every day one day he hit the ball so hart that the wool came out every where so Jackie can't play with it any more. For years later he was big and them he went to the army went he got on the bus the driver said to him he got to sit at the back of the bus so he went to the back of the bus and sit six year later he was sixteen year old he went to play tennis basball and he got gold medal for every thing he play then he got mery to a girl he was happy ever after

THE END

Courage; the story of Jackie Robinson

by Huy

Once upon a time there lived a boy called Jackie Robinson. He was black and his family was poor. Then, one day he went home. "We've got a surprise for you," said his mum. So his mum gave him a baseball. Jackie liked it very much but it was made out of wool so it was different from other baseballs. Jackie played with it every day. One day he hit the ball so hard that the wool came out everywhere. So Jackie can't play with it any more. So he went home.

Four years later he was big and then he went to the army. When he got on the bus the driver said to him that he had to sit at the back of the bus, so he went to the back of the bus and sat. Six years later he was sixteen years old. He went to play tennis and baseball and he got gold medals for everything he played. Then he got married to a girl and he was happy ever after.

The End.

reading it with meaning, so I typed it out for him, correcting his English and separating the segments.

When I returned it to him, he read it through without difficulty. He was obviously pleased with himself. When he read the second segment to me, I asked him what that part had to do with the top part. He was puzzled: "I don't know what I meant". He read it through again, referring to his first draft in Vietnamese. Pointing to the second segment, he said: "I think that was another part of the story. I could cross all that part out. I don't need it."

So he took his pen and put a line through that part. I asked him to read the last segment. "Does it still fit?" I asked, and left him reading and chewing his pen. By the time I returned, he had added extra information, which helped the whole piece follow a better sequence. "Now it makes sense," he said to me. When Huy could distance himself from his writing he could more easily see the parts which had made his meaning confusing in the first place.

Children enjoy learning to edit their work on a word processor.

Helping children to proof-read

Rob Hughes
Sackville Street Public School (NSW)

I sometimes type out the drafts the children write in my Year 6 class in order to help them proof-read more effectively. I do this because the hand-writing of some children is so bad that it gets in the way of them being able to see any mistakes they might have made. I could make them write their work again in neater handwriting, but this would only inhibit their work next time, and I'd only get a few lines. For those children whose handwriting is poor, I find it useful to type their work "warts and all". When I give it back to them, we read the first few lines through together. I ask them to change any unconventionally spelled words, and to under-line any others they are not sure about. The pur-pose of this activity is to get the children to look for, and correct, their own mistakes. That's the first step in proof-reading. I don't expect them to look up all the words they have underlined, as long as they have identified them. When they read their stories in typed form, their own errors of spelling and punctuation become more obvious. For this reason, I believe that writing on the computer, using a word-processor, would produce results in which errors and inconsistencies would be more apparent than they would if the same work had been done in poor-quality handwriting.

And this is the end . . .

Just as children often have difficulty knowing when and how to finish a piece of writing, we, the authors, have experienced the same problems with this book. Over the period we have spent researching and writing, we have constantly been enthused by the exciting strategies we have seen different teachers employing in their classrooms. We have tried to share with the reader as many of these as possible in the space available and, even at this late stage of the book, have discovered other strategies we would like to have included — but we must stop somewhere.

Two areas with which we, and the teachers cited in the book, are not yet completely satisfied are *spelling* and *evaluation*. These teachers seem to be using the most effective strategies in those areas that we have either read about or observed. They are integrating spelling and evaluation into their total language program. It should be obvious, from the many first-hand descriptions contained in this book, that evaluation is, indeed, an inherently continuous part of every classroom activity. However, these teachers are continually seeking more effective ways of addressing these two issues. Much progress has been made, as these "action-researchers" search for the answers.

Teachers must have time and opportunity to try out their ideas, and discuss their findings, just as they need support in their endeavours, if they are to resolve the many questions as yet unanswered. Perhaps their experiences will form the basis of some future book.

Bibliography

Text references and further reading.

Butler, Andrea. *The Story Box in the Classroom, Stage 1.* Rigby Education, Melbourne, 1984.

Chapman, John. *Reading Development and Cohesion.* Heinemann Educational, London, 1983.

Clay, Marie. *Reading; the patterning of complex behaviour.* 2nd edn. Heinemann Educational, Auckland, 1979.

Clay, Marie. *The Early Detection of Reading Difficulties; a diagnostic survey.* 2nd edn. Heinemann Educational, Auckland, 1979.

Graves, Donald H. *Writing; teachers and children at work.* Heinemann Educational, Exeter (New Hampshire), 1983.

Halliday, M.A.K., and Hasan, Raqaiya. *Cohesion in English.* Longman, London, 1976.

Holdaway, Don. *The Foundations of Literacy.* Ashton Scholastic, Gosford, 1979.

Holdaway, Don. *Independence in Reading.* 2nd edn. Ashton Scholastic, Gosford, 1980.

McCracken, Marlene and Robert. *Reading, Writing and Language.* Peguis Publishing, Winnipeg, 1979.

Martin, Bill, and Brogan, Peggy. *Teaching Suggestions for "Sounds Jubilee" and "Sounds Freedom-ring".* Holt, Rinehart and Winston, New York, 1975.

Sloan, Peter, and Latham, Ross. *Teaching Reading Is . . .* Nelson, Melbourne, 1981.

Smith, Frank. *Writing and the Writer.* Heinemann Educational, London, 1982.

Smith, Frank. "Reading like a writer" in *Language Arts* (periodical) 60:5 (1983) pages 558-567. National Council of Teachers of English, Urbana (Illinois).

Tierney, Robert, and Pearson, David P. "Towards a composing model of reading" in *Language Arts* (periodical) 60:5 (1983) pages 568-580. National Council of Teachers of English, Urbana (Illinois).

Turbill, Jan, ed. *No Better Way to Teach Writing!* Primary English Teaching Association, Sydney, 1982.

Turbill, Jan. *Now We Want to Write!* Primary English Teaching Association, Sydney, 1983.

Walshe, R.D., *Every Child Can Write!* Primary English Teaching Association, Sydney, 1981.

Walshe, R.D., ed. *Teaching Literature.* Primary English Teaching Association, Sydney, 1983.

Walshe, R.D., ed. *Donald Graves in Australia; "Children want to write . . ."* Primary English Teaching Association, Sydney, 1981.

Wilson, Lorraine. *Write Me a Sign; about language experience.* Nelson, Melbourne, 1979.

Children's books

Bibliographies compiled by
Denise Ryan

Shared book experience

Allen, Pamela. *Who sank the boat?* Nelson.

Bonne, Rose. *I Know an Old Lady*. Ashton Scholastic.

Burningham, John. *ABC*. Cape.

Carle, Eric. *The Very Hungry Caterpillar*. Puffin.

Charlip, Remy. *What Good Luck, What Bad Luck!* Ashton Scholastic.

Eastman, P.D. *Are You My Mother?* Collins.

Einsel, Walter. *Did You Ever See?* Ashton Scholastic.

Emberley, Barbara. *Drummer Hoff*. Puffin.

Gag, Wanda. *Millions of Cats*. Puffin.

Galdone, Paul. *The Little Red Hen*. World's Work.

Grimm, J. and W. *The Wolf and the Seven Little Kids*. Oxford University Press.

Hutchins, Pat. *Don't Forget The Bacon*. Puffin.

Keats, Ezra Jack. *Over in the Meadow*. Scholastic Press.

Lear, Edward. *The Owl and the Pussycat*. Transworld.

Martin, Bill. *Brown Bear, Brown Bear*. Holt, Rinehart and Winston.

Mayer, Mercer. *What Do You Do With a Kangaroo?* Ashton Scholastic.

Sueling, Barbara. *The Teeny Tiny Woman*. Puffin.

Sutton, Eve. *My Cat Likes to Hide in Boxes*. Puffin.

Tolstoy, Alexei. *The Great Big Enormous Turnip*. Ashton Scholastic.

Books to be read to children K-3

Allen, Pamela. *Who Sank the Boat?* Nelson.

——— *Mr Archimedes' Bath*. Collins.

Armitage, R. AND D. *The Lighthouse Keeper's Lunch*. Puffin.

Breinberg, Petronella. *Sean's Red Bike*. Puffin.

Burningham, John. *Would You Rather?* Oxford University Press.

——— *Trubloff, the mouse who wanted to play the balalaika*. Cape.

——— *Borka, the goose with no feathers*. Cape.

——— *Mr Gumpy's Outing*. Puffin.

Carle, Eric. *The Very Hungry Caterpillar*. Puffin.

Dahl, Roald. *The Enormous Crocodile*. Puffin.

Foreman, Michael. *Dinosaurs and All That Rubbish*. Puffin.

Grimm, J. and W. *Thorn Rose*. Puffin.

Haviland, Virginia. *The Mother Goose Treasury*. Puffin.

Hughes, Shirley. *Dogger*. Bodley Head.

Hutchins, Pat. *Titch*. Puffin.

——— *Rosie's Walk*. Puffin.

——— *Don't Forget the Bacon*. Puffin.

Kent, Jack. *The Fat Cat*.

Lear, Edward. *The Quangle-Wangle's Hat*. Puffin.

Paterson, A.B. *Mulga Bill's Bicycle*. Collins.

Rosen, Michael. *You Can't Catch Me!* Puffin.

Roughsey, Dick. *The Rainbow Serpent*. Collins.

——— *The Giant Devil Dingo*. Collins.

Ryan, John. *Captain Pugwash* (series). Puffin.

Scott-Mitchell, Clare. *When a Goose Meets a Moose*. Methuen.

Sendak, Maurice. *Where the Wild Things Are*. Puffin.

Seuling, Barbara. *The Teeny Tiny Woman*. Puffin.

Sutton, Eve. *My Cat Likes To Hide In Boxes*. Puffin.

Ungerer, Tomi. *The Three Robbers*. Puffin.

Viorst, Judith. *Alexander and the Terrible, Horrible, No Good, Very Bad Day*. Angus and Robertson.

Wagner, Jenny. *The Bunyip of Berkeley's Creek*. Puffin.

Wagner, Jenny. *John Brown, Rose and the Midnight Cat*. Puffin.
— — — *Aranea*. Puffin.

Picture-story books for older children, Years 4-6.

Burningham, John. *Around the World in Eighty Days*. Cape.
Dahl, Roald. *Revolting Rhymes*. Puffin.
Foreman, Michael. *Panda's Puzzle*. Hamish Hamilton.
— — — *Trick-a-Tracker*. Gollancz.
— — — *Long Neck and Thunder Foot*. Kestrel.
— — — *Moose*. Puffin.
— — — *Dinosaurs and All That Rubbish*. Puffin.
Garfield, Leon. *Fair's Fair*. Macdonald.
Greenwood, Ted. *Everlasting Circle*. Hutchinson.
Hoban, Russell. *How Tom Beat Captain Najork and His Hired Sportsmen*. Cape.
Keeping, Charles. *Joseph's Yard*. Oxford University Press.
— — — *The Highwayman* (Alfred Noyes). Oxford University Press.
— — — *Beowulf*. Oxford University Press.
Macarthur-Onslow, Annette. *Uhu*. Ure Smith.
Roughsey, Dick. *The Giant Devil Dingo*. Collins.
Smith, Ivan. *Death of a Wombat*. Sun Books.
— — — *Dingo King*. Sun Books.
Thiele, Colin. *Storm Boy*. Rigby.
— — — *Magpie Island*. Rigby.
Turska, Krystyna. *The Magician of Cracow*. Hamish Hamilton.
Ungerer, Tomi. *Zerelda's Ogre*. Methuen.
— — — *No Kiss For Mother*. Methuen.
— — — *The Beast of Monsieur Racine*. Puffin.
— — — *The Hat*. Puffin.

A few poetry books

Beer, John and Gillian. *Delights and Warnings*. Macdonald.
Cole, William. *Oh, What Nonsense!* Methuen.
Dahl, Roald. *Revolting Rhymes*. Cape/Puffin.
Factor, June. *Far Out, Brussel Sprout!* Oxford University Press.
Haviland, Virginia. *The Mother Goose Treasury*. Puffin.
Heylen, Jill. *Someone is Flying Balloons*. Omnibus.
MacLeod, Doug. *In the Garden of Bad Things*. Kestrel.
Mappin, Alf. *Sing in Bright Colours*. Westbooks.
— — — *Taking in the Sun*. Westbooks.
Martin, Bill. *Sounds of Language* (series). Holt, Rinehart and Winston.
Peguero, Leone. *Poetry Speaks*. Heinemann.
Prelutsky, Jack. *Nightmares; poems to trouble your sleep*. Black.
Rosen, Michael. *You Tell Me*. Puffin.
Scott-Mitchell, Clare. *When a Goose Meets a Moose*. Methuen.

Index